TODAY'S RAILWAYS REVIEW OF THE YEAR

VOLUME 2

DAVID CARTER
PETER FOX

▲1988 saw two very interesting line-ups of locomotives and trains. At the National Railway Museum, York three of Sir Nigel Gresley's A4 pacifics were lined up on 2nd July. The above photograph shows (from left to right) Nos. 4498 *SIR NIGEL GRESLEY*, '2509 *SILVER LINK*' and 4468 *MALLARD*. 'SILVER LINK' is in reality No. 60019 *BITTERN* which had been specially painted in the original grey livery carried by the first four A4s.
Brian Dobbs

▼A line-up of a different kind was provided by the DB on the occasion of the official opening of the *Neubaustrecke* between Fulda and Würzburg on 27th May. The photograph was taken on the approach to Würzburg where the new tracks run parallel with the old tracks. From left to right are Class 50 2–10–0 No. 50 622, Class 601 ex-TEE diesel train with power cars 601 019-3 and 601 014-4, the ICE and Class 120 Bo–Bo electric No. 120 102-9. All tracks are bi-directionally signalled, and all four trains were in motion!
DB

CONTENTS

Britain's Railways in 1988 5
The Political Scene 5
The Channel Tunnel 7
Catering 7
Routes 8
Accidents 9
InterCity 14
Provincial 21
Network SouthEast 29
Railfreight 39
Parcels 57
Locomotives 59
Coaching Stock 71
Technology 80
BR Miscellany 82
Preservation 91
London Underground 111
Light Rail Transit 114
European Scene 118
A Glimpse of Ireland 130
A Railway Diary of 1988 131
BR Stock Changes 1988 141
BR Namings & Denamings 144

Edited by David Carter and Peter Fox.

Written by David Brown, David Carter, Peter Fox, Brian Garvin, Paul Jackson, Colin Marsden, Les Nixon and Paul Shannon with additional contributions from Roger Butcher and Neil Webster.

Published by Platform 5 Publishing Ltd., Lydgate House, Lydgate Lane, Sheffield S10 5FH.

Typesetting by Nicolette Williamson.

Printed by Amadeus Press, Huddersfield, England & Maxwell Data Management, Slack Lane, Derby, England.

ISBN 0 906579 92 9

Further copies of this book may be obtained from Platform 5 Publishing Ltd. at the address shown above. Please enclose 10% of purchase price (UK) or 20% (abroad) to cover postage and packing.

Volume 1 (1987) is also still available at the same price (£11.95) plus postage and packing.

Title page: The solitary Class 89 No. 89001 leaves Doncaster on 5th August with the 11.23 to King's Cross. TDM-fitted HST power car 43013 is providing electric power for train air conditioning and lighting. 91003 can be seen in the background for crew training. *David A. Masterman*

▼After running several railtours in the Salisbury area, Class 8F 2–8–0 No. 48151 and 'West Country' Class 4–6–2 No. 34092 CITY OF WELLS with support coach 21256 call at Bristol Temple Meads for water on their way to Butterley in the early hours of 25th July. *Graham Scott-Lowe*

From the Publisher

This second volume of Today's Railways Review of the Year covers the most important events of the year 1988 for British Rail, London Underground, light rail and railway preservation together with the major events in Europe.

The book has been produced by David Carter and Peter Fox. Unfortunately Steven Knight left Platform 5 during January 1989, after the dust jackets had been printed, and these, therefore, incorrectly carry his name as an author. Steven's leaving meant that the production of this book was delayed, as it was not until later in the year, when David Carter joined us, that work could commence on putting the book together. Unfortunately certain other time-sensitive projects had to be undertaken first, i.e. our book 'Midland Railway Portrait' had to be produced for Midland Counties 150, the 'Benelux' book had to be produced for NS 150 and the 'Summer Special' had to be produced for the summer. This meant that the production of this book had to be put back still further. We can only apologise for this late publication, and will make every effort to ensure that Volume 3 will be much earlier. Please note that in order not to disappoint customers, we have decided that Volume 3 will not be advertised until it is actually at the printers.

We would like to thank all contributors and photographers who have helped with this book, also the publicity departments of BR HQ, Network SouthEast, InterCity, Railfreight, the Eastern and Southern Regions, GMPTE, SYPTE, Strathclyde PTE, WYPTE, DLR, SNCF, DB, BREL, the Department of Transport, the TUCCs, the London Regional Passengers Committee and Transport 2000. No thanks are due to BR Anglia and Scottish Regions who provided us with no information whatsoever, despite repeated requests.

DAVID CARTER (Editor)

PETER FOX (Publisher and Editor)

REVIEW OF THE YEAR VOLUME 3

Contributions for Volume Three, covering 1989, will be most welcome. Good quality black and white photographs and colour transparencies (previously unpublished please) reflecting important events and developments should be securely packed with the name of the photographer on each slide or transparency and sent to the following address:

Today's Railways – Review of the Year Vol.3,
Platform 5 Publishing Ltd.,
Lydgate House,
Lydgate Lane,
Sheffield, S10 5FH

Preparation of the next edition has already started, and contributors should submit the bulk of their work as soon as possible (other than important items which occur later in the year).

▼An unusual diversion occurred on 14th February. Due to overunning of engineering work, loco-hauled Sheffield–Liverpool trains were diverted via Chinley South Junction, Peak Forest, Buxton and the LNWR route to Hazel Grove. This diversion is unlikely to be repeated as the Class 156 units which now work the service are out of gauge on the LNWR branch. Class 31/4 No. 31453 breasts the summit at Peak Forest on the former Derby–Manchester line with the 13.59 Sheffield–Liverpool. *Les Nixon*

BRITAIN'S RAILWAYS IN 1988

THE POLITICAL SCENE

Transport matters in general, and overcrowding in particular, moved to the forefront of political debate by the end of 1988, topics such as defence being relegated. Increased personal mobility, combined with the fact that Britain is relatively small and densely-populated, meant that congestion of one sort or another would emerge as an issue sooner or later. Whether packed like sardines on the 06.32 Ipswich to Blackpool, crawling around the M25 – London's orbital car park as it has come to be known – or waiting hours for a delayed holiday flight, the root cause was the same: congestion, mostly at peak times, but increasingly during the 'shoulder periods', because of inadequate facilities.

Any year provides contrasts between the good and bad news. The contrasts were somehow greater in 1988. On one hand continued progress with the Channel Tunnel, record levels of investment, completion of electrification to Leeds, increased passenger demand and a re-invigorated Provincial network; on the other, continued deliberation over the Settle–Carlisle line and a spate of passenger train accidents, the worst at Clapham claiming 35 lives. Overcrowding on the railways had been simmering as an issue all year in certain parts of the country – particularly the South East and West Yorkshire. It took the tragedy of Clapham, partly fuelled by the somewhat opportunistic statements of the Opposition, to put overcrowding firmly on the agenda.

The various Transport Users Consultative Committees all spoke of overcrowding as a worsening problem. Also, whilst welcoming the various performance targets established by BR in 1987 (such as punctuality, train cleaning and speed of telephone enquiry response), reservation was expressed that figures for load factors (degree of overcrowding) only applied to Network SouthEast.

1988 was a time of further change within the government itself. On policy, the government acknowledged for the first time in public that it was considering railway privatisation. On 20th June, Sir David Mitchell said in the Commons that his department: "is discussing long-term options with BR ... having regard to the need for systems of regulation and subsidy for loss-making services".

By October the press were reporting options under government scrutiny including selling BR off to regional companies; by present business structure, as a whole (as BR plc) or with separate track and operating authorities.

Pro-rail David Mitchell himself did not last very long. In a cabinet reshuffle revealed on 26th July, he was replaced by the youthful Michael Portillo. Only 35, he has risen through the ranks quickly, has been a government whip and personal secretary to the secretary of state for transport. With his Enfield Southgate constituency just down the road from Mrs Thatcher's at Finchley, he was every bit a 'Thatcherite'.

The secretary of state for transport, Paul Channon, looked increasingly uncomfortable in the wake of disasters like Clapham, Lockerbie, and during the King's Cross inquiry. He lacked self-projection. Being Mrs Thatcher's sixth transport secretary – in a line of undistinguished holders of the post – his job was far from secure. Little more than a year after his appointment, rumours started to circulate about his future. More a traditional 'Heathite' Tory than a 'Thatcherite', he did manage to say the right things in the right places occasionally. At the 1988 Conservative party conference he put forward ideas to open up roads, railways, bridges, ports, buses and municipal airports to the private sector and, he hoped, more competition. One comment was: "If it moves, privatise it".

Mr Channon and Mr Portillo both suffer from the long-term nature of transport planning and construction. Whether it is congestion on the M25 or on the East Coast Main Line, they endured criticism of decisions rarely made by them but rather by predecessors; although both have increasingly important and difficult jobs, only Mr Portillo did not appear to be permanently on the defensive. By the end of 1988, commentators saw the young high-flier as being groomed for greater things.

In the political league table, the environment continued its rise during 1988. Although taught to children for years before in geography lessons, there were suddenly few people unaware of the greenhouse effect, ozone depletion and a host of other problems. With this change in emphasis, it still seemed remarkable that the government's investment criteria still continued to favour roads. Whereas rail investment has to be justified purely by return on capital, for both roads cost benefit analysis discounts cost against environmental benefits, increased safety, reduced journey times etc. Furthermore, road traffic is a major source of the gases which produce acid rain and global warming. During the previous year, vehicle emissions had accounted for 44% of nitrogen oxides, the major cause of acid rain, and 17% of carbon dioxide, the main 'greenhouse' gas.

Parts of the railway environment continued to look worse due to the attentions of the graffiti vandals. An import from the USA, the craze has involved disfiguration of trains, stations and lineside structures. Despite valiant efforts by BR and LUL to clean up the scrawlings (masquerading as 'art') the problem got worse in 1988.

By the end of 1988 there were 23.3 m vehicles in Britain, up 5% on 1987. This dominance of the motor car left us with a traffic density twice that of West Germany, three times that of France. This brings us back to congestion, implicity or explicity mentioned as a problem by BR officials – most, usually as a 'problem of success' – and in the year's two key documents

BR ANNUAL REPORT & ACCOUNTS

The British Rail Annual Report and Accounts 1987/88 reveal clearly which direction the Board is heading. Its paymaster at present, the government, wants to concentrate the cost of using a service – water, electricity, rail travel or whatever – at its user. Subsidies, it thinks, get in the way of the market system. The subsidy to loss-making services or Public Service Obligation (PSO) would, from April 1988, be directed only at Provincial and continue falling in real terms. More of this in a moment.

In physical quantities, the Annual Report highlighted passenger volume up 8% on the previous year at 20.6 billion passenger miles, the highest for 27 years. Furthermore, these people were transported on a certainly leaner, probably fitter, railway. Whilst passenger journeys and freight traffic have expanded with the economy, the railway's stock of assets – locomotives, coaching vehicles and freight vehicles – have continued to fall. The switch from a labour-intensive to a relatively capital-intensive railway is plain to see, the Group's rail operations employing 133 567 staff by the end of the period, 14% less than in 1983.

In monetary terms, improved staff productivity, better

▲Major property development is a key feature in the transformation of the railway environment and British Rail's finances. The view shows work in progress on the east side of Liverpool Street station showing part of the Broadgate development. *Dr. Iain Scotchman*

asset utilisation, and lower units costs – such as through radio signalling – are only half the equation, the other being revenue. Real growth in earnings was achieved by all three passenger sectors. Total receipts were 13% higher than in 1986/7 at £1,622 m, the highest total in real terms since nationalisation in 1948. With Railfreight marking its tenth year as a fully commercial sector and showing a good performance, the Group as a whole had a surplus of £113 m, which became a surplus of £291 m after interest and extraordinary items – the latter including healthy contributions from property sales.

Key points for the business sectors were:

InterCity. Gross income at £732.8 m represented a 7% real increase and the highest since InterCity services were introduced 22 years before. In InterCity's last year in receipt of subsidy, the operating loss was reduced by 19% to £86.2 m. The net cost of InterCity On Board Services increased by £4 m to £12 m but, after taking new accounting practices into account, this represented an underlying improvement in performance on the previous year.

Network SouthEast. Gross income was £804.7 m and the operating loss (before interest and government grant) was £169.8 m. The grant to Network SouthEast has been cut by 34% in real terms since 1983.

Provincial. Gross income was £247.2 m and the operating loss (before interest and government grant) was £473.1 m. Real earnings rose a healthy 7% on 1986/7.

Railfreight. Gross income was £555 m, the operating surplus (before interest) £43.6 m. The surplus represented a turnaround, in only 3 years, from losses of £281 m following the 1984/5 miners' strike.

Parcels. Gross income was £120.3 m, the operating loss (before interest) being £6.8 m. Red Star traffic growth offset the loss of newspaper distribution traffic.

Other key results were:

Travellers Fare Ltd. During 1988, status changed to that of a limited company. Gross income was £74.1 m and the operating surplus (before interest) was £7.5 m.

Freightliners Ltd. Gross income was £97.7 m and the operating loss (again, before interest) was £6.2 m.

BREL (1988) Ltd. In the run-up to the autumn transfer of BREL to the private sector, a new wholly-owned BR subsidiary, BREL (1988) was formed on 1st April. Gross income for 1987–8 was £257.5 m.

British Rail Maintenance Ltd. In its first year of operation a gross income of £168.9 m was achieved.

Transmark. Consultancy work on 148 projects in 30 countries around the world produced a gross income for the Board of £4.6 m.

British Rail Property Board. Property sales produced £181.4 m, the gross income from letting was £82.4 m. An operating surplus of £61.4 m was achieved as a result.

The Group result is, of course, after taking the PSO into account. The 1988 Corporate Plan forecasts financial objectives until 1992/3. Amongst the targets set, the PSO must be only 56% of that allowed in 1983. This rate of change was broadly being met by period's end, 31st March. Returning to the original paragraph, the secretary of state for transport denied there was any link between a declining PSO and increasing overcrowding. Mr Channon pointed at record investment in 1988 – £495 m on railway improvements – and the sum of £3.8 billion to be invested during the next 5 years. Being a politician, he played down the price of this investment: a locomotive-hauled train being replaced by a two-car Sprinter, for example. The various performance indicators such as 'average train load' and 'average receipts per train mile' may look very encouraging at Euston House or Marsham Street; when you are standing in the vestibule of a Sprinter with four hours' travel to Blackpool still to go, they do not look so good.

Mr Channon also omitted to mention that the investment concerned was BR's own, financed by borrowing and not a government grant as in the case of road investment.

Returning briefly to property, the Board sees property income from rent and land sale as increasingly important in offsetting the falling government grant. The increasing commercialisation of stations continued apace during 1988. From the way some of Britain's big city stations began to look, travel was certainly the last thing on BR's mind. Waterloo, for instance, has a retail turnover of £80 m per year. The ticket office was to be found between The Sock Shop and Tie Rack. Retail income apart, work continued on the Liverpool Street/Broadgate and Charing Cross office developments.

Wherever you looked in 1988 it was apparent that things were changing fast. From signalling to ticketing, from track maintenance to traction technology, the railway was being prepared for the 1990s. Under the influence of Jane Priestman, BR's director of architecture and design, it began to look the part too. In charge of an in-house design team and working with the cream of private consultancies, the InterCity swallow symbol and Railfreight squadron markings were formulated soon after her appointment in November 1986. Recognising what car companies, textile companies and most others have known for years, BR's philosophy at last became 'design pays'. The 1960s corporate image (and the corporate colours of blue and grey) was quickly disappearing.

THE CHANNEL TUNNEL

As the 1990s approach people's minds finally began to turn to Europe. 1992 was emphasised by the government, the year of the EEC 'single internal market', with supposed free movement of people, goods and services. Inextricably linked, the Channel Tunnel opens just one year later. For many cynics, 1988 marked a realisation that it would be completed and that Britain would finally be linked to the other 264 m Europeans by a high-speed railway.

Returning to contrasts, the cities of the Nord–Pas-de-Calais region of France argued over which route the Paris–London high-speed line would take; all wanted the economic benefits of being part of Europe's high-speed network. In affluent, crowded and conservative Kent no-one seemed to want the link. BR published its plans for the high-speed Channel Tunnel link through Kent on 14th July. Four possible routes had been selected with varying costs and environmental impact assigned to each; London to tunnel-mouth journey times varied greatly depending on the alignment of each route. Spectacular maps quickly appeared in the daily papers, and the Sunday papers in particular. From Acacia Avenue somewhere in the SE London suburbs to quaint villages nestling in the North Downs there were rumblings; ministers, retired brigadiers, young couples about to have their homes 'raised to the ground' were all interviewed by a press engaged in its favourite pastime of knocking BR.

Normally sleepy Kent became the focus for mass meeting, action groups, and rallying points for marches to Number 10. Press sensationalism only made worse the already clumsy handling of the issue by BR.

If Kent's dilemma was which of the four shortlisted routes would be chosen for the high-speed line, the North's and West's problems were, paradoxically, Kent and London. The North of England Regional Consortium, formed in 1981 and consisting of influencial businessmen, together with pressure groups and local authorities, successfully highlighted this point during public meetings in 1988. They stressed that maximum regional gains from the Channel Tunnel could only be attained by removing transport bottlenecks in London and Kent.

Putting the politics to one side for a moment, service tunnel boring started from both ends in early January – this only five months since the Anglo-French Fixed Link Treaty was actually ratified and in which the Eurotunnel concession came into force.

Whilst 1988 saw BR beginning to sort out its plans for the surge in international passenger travel, the first real move in attracting freight was not made until October 1988 with the setting up of Railfreight Distribution under the directorship of Mr Ian Brown. Railfreight had succeeded in recovering from the 1984–5 miners' strike. However, Railfreight Distribution was to: continue progress from a supply-led to a demand-led business, be clearly divided on geographical grounds (Britain, Europe, Ireland, Deep-sea), enhance its image with customers and potential customers and look into better ways of road-rail transferral for Channel Tunnel trains. This was to be achieved by developing regional hubs, such as Doncaster, for such transfers. The tunnel would open only 56 months later so Railfreight would have to move quickly. Some sort of 'Piggyback' system emerged as the best idea for development given the limitations of the British loading gauge. The 1987 report 'Turning Trucks into Trains' had suggested that the benefits of efficient intermodal freight transfer would be enormous – possibly 13–15 tonnes per year.

In 1988 a lorry would typically take 72 hours to transport, say 25 tonnes of freight from Manchester to Milan. If BR could get its act together, by 1993 750 tonnes could be hauled the same distance in exactly half the time. We hope it does because, for all BR's problems, the future looked bright by year's end.

▲One of Hunslet-built Channel Tunnel construction locomotives being transported south down the A1 on 11th August. *Ian Cowley*

CATERING

PROVINCIAL

Provincial's guidelines for its new 'Express' network included the provision of some form of trolley catering service on most trains. This refreshment service is provided on a contract basis by private contractors, Rightline Catering (which has successfully operated on the North Trans Pennine route) were to operate on Anglia–Midlands/NW services and on the Birmingham–Nottingham–Cleethorpes route. It is unfortunate that timetables and publicity only give the broad details of 'trolley service for whole or part of journey'. From the passengers view this is far from satisfactory and details of the points between which the facility is available should be given. It is not uncommon for some East Anglia–North West trains to be devoid of a trolley service between Ely and Chesterfield.

INTERCITY

On InterCity the 'Cuisine 2000' concept began to show some shortfalls, especially in the quantities of food taken on board at the start of the journey. The full menu was not always available. Whilst the steak proved popular and was often sold out most passengers didn't know whether to put gravy or custard onto the turkey and apricot pie. In August InterCity On Board Services (ICOBS), as the train catering organisation is now known, launched a new range of pre-packed sandwiches with up to 10 different fillings. Despite its shortcomings, ' Cuisine 2000' had spread to all WCML services from May, except the Euston–Inverness 'The Clansman' and the Euston–Holyhead boat trains.

Towards the end of the year ICOBS announced that 'open sandwiches' prepared on the train would again be available in some restaurant and buffet cars. To avoid any irregularities in the quantity of filling contained in the sandwiches, one reason why they were withdrawn from sale in the past, the fillings will come as pre-packed portions.

The popular 'Cross-Country Grill' continued to be available on selected services but changes in menu limited the meals that could be purchased.

In July, the decision was taken to remove from sale cigarettes and cigars from InterCity buffet cars. British Rail announced that it had taken the decision in order to better utilise the limited shelf space available in train buffet cars.

STATION CATERING

Following the issue of tender documents in October last year, it was announced in January that the British Rail subsidiary, Travellers Fare Limited, had been successful in winning 68 of the 96 station sites. A further 7 sites were withdrawn as a result of new development opportunities at the sites.

On 3rd June, with the approval of the Secretary of State for Transport British Rail invited tenders for the Travellers Fare business. Because Travellers Fare was the most successful tenderer, in the earlier round, retaining 70% of the sites offered in 1987, the British Railways Board abandoned its plan to offer further station catering sites through individual tender.

On 20th December the announcement was made to the effect that Travellers Fare Limited had been sold to a management 'buy-out' consortium. British Rail, therefore, becomes landlord and receives rent on the use of 270 catering units at over 140 stations.

ROUTES

1988 saw the closure of the Radstock branch (from Marcroft Wagon Works to Hapsford (Somerset Quarry Junction). Two months later, on 30th August, the Oakamoor branch (from British Industrial Sand's works to Leek Brook Junction) in Staffordshire closed. On 15th October the line from Trafford Park Junction to Gorton Junction in Manchester was closed, a line that had been used for freight and diverted Sunday trains, particularly East Anglia–North West services.

In Strathclyde, the Maunchline–Annbank line was re-opened to freight traffic on 17th March. Mid-Glamorgan saw an expanded passenger rail network with the re-opening of the Cynon Valley line on 2nd October.

Two parts of the BR network deserve particular analysis, namely the Settle–Carlisle line and the Trowell Junction–Lenton Junction line.

SETTLE–CARLISLE

Six years after BR stopped operating through Nottingham–Leeds–Glasgow trains, and five years after the formal closure proposal, the battle both continued and intensified. The government emphasised that it saw the threatened line as a heritage and tourism-based railway, not one for service trains or to cater directly for enthusiasts. The tourist railway, transport minister David Mitchell explained, was better suited to private sector operation. After all, only 20% of travellers on the Settle–Carlisle line were local users travelling to work or shopping. The rest were tourists. David Mitchell and environment secretary Nicholas Ridley emphasised this point. The transport minister spelled out what he thought BR's role was on 16th May, the day BR was asked to find a private buyer. "BR's priority is to invest in a modern rail system for the 21st century, not provide pleasure rides for railway archaeologists".

The 16th May was the day that David Mitchell said that the government was "minded" to consent to closure of the line.

An offer of local authority financial assistance to help

▶The Settle–Carlisle line has proved itself as a diversionary route and as a line with considerable tourism potential. The Easter period saw particularly frequent diversions of Anglo–Scottish InterCity services via the Settle–Carlisle. Providing an unusual sight on this line, power car 43099 heads a St. Pancras–Carlisle excursion at Helwith Bridge on 3rd December. Excursions by HST have become increasingly frequent over recent years. They generally attract a wider clientele than more traditional railtours. InterCity and Hertfordshire Railtours began a jointly-marketed programme of railtours in 1988 which brought HSTs to such unusual destinations as Kingswear, Blackpool and Whitby. *Les Nixon*

BR repair Ribblehead Viaduct was rejected by the government as not as helpful as it seems. The government ensured potential private buyers knew what help they were entitled to: a £1 m grant from English Heritage for Ribblehead Viaduct, a £100,000 grant from the Rural Development Commission and a £100,000 grant from the Countryside Commission for the viaduct, train services, marketing initiatives, tourism projects, etc. Lazard Brothers issued a prospectus in June. Initial press reports indicated considerable private interest but, as the year went on, it became apparent that few operators would be able to handle the 72 mile route.

BR continued to promote the line, its declared policy to maximise revenue before closure continuing. In May it issued 500,000 promotional leaflets in time to attract more summer tourists. Passenger demand increased further during the year with even some strengthened trains experiencing overcrowding.

The anti-closure campaigners became even more effective. Backed by one consultant's report about the 'cascading' of HSTs from other routes to form a fast Leeds/Bradford–Glasgow through service, the campaigners claimed the line could earn £1 m a year. Whilst the Settle–Carlisle line's tourism and diversionary advantages continued to be apparent during 1988, another possibility was mooted: the route could form part of a through Channel Tunnel freight route between Kent and Scotland - the idea being similar to a Kent–Liverpool (docks) 'landbridge' line, also being proposed.

By the end of 1988 the Settle–Carlisle line was as much a household name as the 'greenhouse effect', and the press had begun to say that, one way or another, the spectacular line would be saved.By the end of the year, a decision was still awaited.

TROWELL JUNCTION–LENTON JUNCTION

An interesting closure proposal was the subject of a TUCC inquiry in Nottingham on 19th May. The proposal under discussion was the closure of the line from Trowell Junction on the Midland Erewash Valley line to Lenton Junction, Nottingham via Radford. The route was scheduled to be used by one InterCity train per day in each direction, but in fact many Provincial North West–East Anglia trains used the line, especially when running late, as the route is five minutes quicker than the longer route via Toton which these trains are scheduled to use. BR's case was that since the trains routed via Radford were no quicker (because of pathing time – ed!) there was no case for keeping the route open! This argument did not go down too well with the objectors, nor with the chairman of the committee. Before the committee's report was published, the route was closed prematurely by a freight train derailment at Trowell. Plain track was substituted for the junction on to the passenger lines pending the committee's decision. However, later in the year, BR announced the good news that a change in policy meant the line would reopen for Provincial Express services, but not until 1990. The bad news was that they were to run from Nottingham to Peterborough via Melton Mowbray which would wipe out the time advantage gained by going via Trowell.

ACCIDENTS

As mentioned in the introduction to this book, 1988 was a bad year for accidents. Strangely, the first six covered here did not occur until June, the rest following closely behind. The worst, at Clapham, occurred in a tragic run-up to Christmas alongside the earthquake in Armenia (50,000 dead) and the plane crash at Lockerbie (280 dead).

14th JUNE, COPYHOLD JUNCTION, HAYWARDS HEATH, WEST SUSSEX

Class 56 loco No. 56062 was derailed on the Ardingley branch (next to the London–Brighton line) whilst hauling empty stone wagons to Westbury, Wiltshire. The locomotive plunged down the 40 ft embankment and landed on its side. Luckily the driver and guard were unhurt. After a 3½ month salvage operation, 56062 was lifted (minus the 33 ton power unit, bogies and roof section – recovered later) back on to waiting bogies on the line.

21st AUGUST, HYNDLAND, GLASGOW

The driver, two other crew members and a passenger were taken to hospital when the 10.25 Balloch to Motherwell EMUs derailed after pulling out of Jordanhill station. The train, with 56 passengers on board, had been travelling eastwards towards the city centre. The wheels of the front coach of the 6-coach train left the track with the coach ending up across the adjacent track. No other train was involved.

28th OCTOBER, CRICKLEWOOD, NORTH LONDON

During the small hours of this Friday morning, two close-coupled locomotives started to roll along along sidings. Class 31s Nos. 31202 (leading) and 31236 crashed through the headshunt and down on to the road 40 feet below. The dual carriageway road is part of the North London circular road which meets the southern end of the M1 nearby. The location – Staples Corner – becomes very congested as soon

▼The remarkable scene at Cricklewood on 28th October. This incident made the front pages of several national newspapers, it making a sensational photograph and a good 'story': runaway locos in mystery plunge, etc!
Brian Morrison

▲56062 lies at the foot of the embankment at Copyhold Junction after having had its engine removed. The date is 4th September.
Alex Dasi-Sutton

◀Crowds look on as the emergency services survey the damage at Hyndland. *Press Association*

▶▲▲The mangled front of the Blackpool–Liverpool Sprinter, in which the driver was killed on 11th November. *Press Association*

▶▲A Class 47 tows the stricken Sprinter away.
The St. Helens Reporter

▶The scene near Newcastle's King Edward Bridge on 30th November.
Press Association

as the morning rush hour starts. Commuting motorists were startled to see the trailing locomotive (uncoupled in the accident) hanging precariously from the headshunt above, resting on the broken back of 31202.

In a delicate rescue operation the trailing locomotive was lifted back on to the sidings by a 300-ton road crane (used in the 1986 Colwich accident). A Class 47 and a Class 31 assisted by pulling 31236 from behind. With its underframe broken, No. 31202 was cut up on site and traffic was flowing again by the Saturday morning. Two private firms and BR staff at Willesden were involved in the difficult operation.

11th NOVEMBER, ST. HELENS, MERSEYSIDE

The driver was killed when his Class 150/2 Sprinter No. 52209 was derailed causing the DMU to crash into the centre pier of an overbridge shortly after leaving St. Helens station on the 22.10 Blackpool–Liverpool service. The train had been travelling at 20 mph and 16 people were injured. A week before this accident, a colleague of the editor had travelled along this stretch of line and reported a particularly rough ride.

30th NOVEMBER, NEWCASTLE

Two HSTs collided on the northern approach to the King Edward Bridge over the River Tyne. The 14.52 Aberdeen–King's Cross passed through a set of points when the 16.00 King's Cross–Aberdeen struck the southbound train's rear-most carriages, one of which was overturned. The power car of the northbound train was severely damaged. Thirteen passengers were injured, none seriously though. Later, repairs were due to be effected on the nose of the (north-bound train's) power car, No. 43047.

12th DECEMBER, CLAPHAM, LONDON

The story started the night before. Vandals placed a concrete mixer on the line at Parkstone, between Bournemouth and Poole. This derailed the front carriage of an early evening Waterloo–Weymouth 'Wessex Electric' service. The Class 442 concerned was No. 2417. This unit had been scheduled to work the 06.14 Bournemouth–Waterloo the following morning.

On Monday 12th December, what should have been a train formed of Class 442 units (which have integrally-constructed bodies) was formed by a replacement Mark 1-based Class 432/438 (4 Rep/4TC) formation. It started its journey from Bournemouth rather than Poole and set off at 06.30. By the time this 12-coach train reached Clapham it was carrying 468 passengers. It ran into the back of the stationary 07.18 Basingstoke–Waterloo, a 12-coach Class 423 (4 Vep) just south of Clapham Junction station. The 07.18 was carrying no less than 906 passengers. One passenger, BR financial planning manager, Provincial, Peter Bassett described the collision as "an almighty bang and then silence". An ECS train, the 8-coach 08.03 Waterloo–Hazlemere then struck the debris scattered over the adjacent line.

The guard of the empty train ran forward along the line to warn an approaching commuter train. The driver of the 07.18 train meanwhile contacted signalmen, who called the emergency services. At 8.13 am the first 999 call was received by the emergency services. Four London hospitals were put on red alert. The first fire engine was on the scene at 8.17 am and the first ambulance at 8.21 am.

Teachers and pupils from the school next to the cutting clambered down the cutting to help the injured. By 10.00, 50 ambulances and 15 fire engines as well as hordes of press reporters and cameramen were at Clapham. Southern Region general manager, Gordon Pettitt took charge of the railway aspect of the rescue operation. Shortly afterwards, BR chairman Bob Reid, transport secretary Paul Channon, and transport minister Michael Portillo visited the site.

BR switchboards were jammed all day with calls coming from anxious friends, relatives and the press. By 13.00 all live casualties were freed from the wreckage and taken to hospital. The death toll later rose to 35. Amongst the victims was the driver of the 06.30 from Bournemouth, another experienced driver, and another driver in the cab with him; this driver had been travelling to Waterloo for a normal driving turn later that morning.

Once the victims were evacuated, work to clear the lines started in earnest. Using a 75 ton rail crane from Stewarts Lane, a 76 ton rail crane from East Wimbledon and two privately-owned 300 ton road cranes, coaches were re-railed. Some vehicles needed to be placed on accommodation bogies. Badly-damaged coaches were lifted by road onto low loaders and taken by road to Stewarts Lane. BR teams worked with a LUL back-up team equipped with cutting equipment.

Train services were diverted or cancelled but, gradually, things returned to normal. Two slow lines were clear to traffic by the start of the Tuesday evening rush hour with the two fast lines clear by Wednesday.

In contrast to the long and painful recrimination, investigation and recommendation following the King's Cross Underground disaster (which occurred on 18th November 1987), BR quickly admitted responsibility.

Payments of £2,000 and funeral expenses were made to relatives without delay. BR also set up an internal inquiry to quickly establish the cause of the accident and prevent a repetition.

◄The response of the emergency services was acknowledged to be quick and efficient. Soon after the crash, firemen use cutting equipment to clear tangled wreckage. The cold early-morning light highlights the severity of the impact. *Daily Express*

►BR chairman, Sir Robert Reid (visible, bottom left) was also soon on the scene, as was SR general manager Gordon Pettitt. Heavy lifting equipment was in situ by this time. *Press Association*

▼Twenty-four hours after the crash the site was almost clear. *Brian Morrison*

THE CLAPHAM AFTERMATH

The accident was the worst on BR since that in 1967 at Hither Green in which 49 died. Early judgement – less than 10 hours after the crash – in the internal inquiry revealed that faulty installation of equipment associated with the £20 m Waterloo Area Resignalling Scheme was responsible. Accidents resulting from signal failures are relatively rare – 96% of train accidents (collisions, derailments, etc.) are caused by other factors.

A public inquiry was announced in parliament. As all interests have to represented it takes longer to organise and was scheduled to open in February 1989. As the Railway Inspectorate (part of the Department of Transport) is responsible for checking track and signalling installations, unusually, an independent inspector was appointed to handle the public inquiry.

The Transport Act 1962 – one of the four sources from which BR broadly derives its statutory and financial duties – says the Board should "have due regard ... to efficiency, economy and safety of operation". Wider questions that the Clapham disaster posed concern the safety/economy dilemma. Accidents will always happen. If they are to be minimised there is a financial cost. The number of deaths from car accidents indicates that, given the personal freedom a car allows, people will sacrifice some safety in favour of faster journeys and lower cost.

Opposition transport spokesman John Prescott misguidedly attacked overcrowding, and mentioned the age of the stock involved. On the latter point, the Bournemouth train would have been formed of Mark 3-based stock but for the attentions of the vandals the night before. Having proved itself at Colwich, Morpeth and Northallerton, the Mark 3 might have saved more lives at Clapham. Overcrowding can just worsen the consequences of an accident and is not a cause of it.

As the year closed other questions to be addressed emerged: are S & T staff working too long under too much pressure?; do BR S & T staff work effectively with contractors also involved with the resignalling?; are more cab radios needed?; should safety be included in railway investment appraisals, e.g. the greater collision resistance of modern coaches?

Perhaps what John Prescott should have been attacking was congestion of an overstretched, under-resourced network, not overcrowding on the fated trains.It soon became clear how many key staff were being over-stretched too. The public inquiry would have its work cut out.

INTERCITY

A new timetable launch is often a good background for an up-beat message. Announcing the May timetable changes, Simon Fraser, InterCity manager, Eastern, said: "Now that government support has been withdrawn, InterCity must achieve a financial turnaround of £102 m in just two years. When related to turnover, that's faster than the recent turnarounds made by British Airways, British Steel, ICI and Courtaulds. We are bang on target".

The timetable was adjusted so that an improved frequency over 'core' sections (eg. Bristol–York or St. Pancras–Leicester) would be offered. Off-peak, the story was one of rationalisation (e.g. that to the Sleeper services). In contrast to the 'jumbo' trains on Western Region holiday services a few years earlier, we had short-formation trains on the North East–South West route from May 1988; usually loaded to 6 coaches, these loco-hauled trains were designed to provide HST-type average speeds over the Leeds–Bristol section (where HSTs cannot take advantage of their 125 mph capability).

A trend that continued in 1988 was for earlier InterCity departures and not only for London-bound trains. Named in connection with the Armada 400 celebrations, the 'Armada' provided a fast, much-needed early morning service each way between Leeds and Plymouth. The first northbound service, however, was a total disaster.

Through services between Liverpool and the South West were re-introduced. Out of favour were the cross-London InterCity services, being pruned to just a Manchester–Brighton return and a Liverpool–Dover return; all these stopped en route at Birmingham. Still trying to capitalise on the potential demand in the wealthy Thames Valley, a new 'Sussex Scot' was introduced from Edinburgh/Glasgow to Brighton, travelling via the WCML, Birmingham, Coventry, Reading, Kensington, E. Croydon and Gatwick. 'The Northumbrian' (Newcastle–Reading–Bournemouth) was also introduced. The Newcastle–Poole service gained the name 'The Northumbrian'.

The Manchester–Scotland services were expanded, and Derby and Sheffield were linked to Edinburgh by a through train once more. This was achieved by extending 'The Cornishman' HST north of Newcastle.

For the first time all through trains to and from Newquay were HSTs. On the other hand the lack of provision for the thousands travelling to the NEC for Motor Show '88 was incredible. Packed service trains were order of the day. It is at events such as this that it is apparent how lean the 'leaner and fitter' BR had become!

The frequency of the North East–South West service was improved slightly in 1988 but despite publicity suggesting that the Sheffield–Birmingham service was to be hourly, a totally irregular service was provided with certain large gaps. The haphazard timetable caused pathing problems for provincial services at Sheffield. Reliability was poor also. For the period of the summer timetable 'The Armada' HST was replaced by the 'generator set' (i.e. locomotive, generator coach, HST Mark 3 coaches and brake van) on numerous occasions – 6 times northbound, 8 times southbound. On the occasions on which the 'The Armada' operated like this, as an HST with only one operational power car, or by standard loco-hauled train the average delay was 28 minutes. Other trains also saw substitutions of hauled stock from time to time.

On the East Coast Main Line there were general reductions in journey times; Aberdeen was under 7 hours' travel from London for the first time by 'The Flying Scotsman' and 'The Aberdonian'.

On the West Coast Main Line, there were few service changes. Hartford was given a bigger role as a railhead for North Cheshire with some Liverpool–London trains and the Liverpool–West of England trains calling there.

On the Midland Main Line, an extra HST set was provided, and this enabled the provision of a timetable of regular half-hourly off-peak departures from London to Leicester, with a train every 90 minutes to Nottingham and one every 90 minutes terminating at Leicester. Certain 'fast' trains called at Luton for Thameslink service. Unfortunately, most off-peak trains were actually slowed down between Leicester and St. Pancras due to extra recovery allowances!

The new timetable attracted much criticism from organisations in Sheffield because of the lack of an hourly service and the extended journey times caused by the stopping of Sheffield trains at various stations between Leicester and Luton. The 08.17 train from Sheffield came in for particular criticism. Equivalent trains to this in previous timetables had always been very popular, both for first class business travel and second class optional travel. The train was decelerated with six stops and actually took as long as was previously the case with Class 45 haulage and Mark 2 stock! To make matters worse, the Restaurant Car was withdrawn, with first class passengers not taking kindly to having the inferior grill menu served by staff who could not cope with the demand. The Restaurant Car was eventually restored to this service, but not advertised!

The only loco-hauled trains in the new timetable consisted of one train each way on Mondays and Fridays between Derby and St. Pancras. Because of overcrowding in the peak hours, an additional Mondays–Fridays Derby–St. Pancras loco-hauled working was introduced with the October timetable. This was diagrammed on most days for the remaining 'Peak' No. 45106, but on most days the train was 47-hauled, often with one of the departmentally numbered examples. A press conference in Sheffield later on in the year gave hope for better services in the future, however. Faster trains were promised in 1989, an hourly service in 1990 and an eventual 2-hour timing between Sheffield and London.

SILVER STANDARD

On 1st February InterCity launched its 'Silver Standard' facility on key business trains on the Liverpool–London route. This enables passengers with a full price standard class ticket to join specifically-identified coaches on the train. Free seat reservations are provided and a steward is on hand throughout the journey to provide complimentary refreshments and serve other meals.

The aim of 'Silver Standard' is to cater for the needs of people who use standard class for business. At the end of the year InterCity reported that business revenue on the Liverpool 'Silver Standard' service had increased by 20%.

LEISURE PULLMAN

For the summer timetable, commencing 16th May, a series of daytime leisure Pullman services were operated. These ran until 30th September and utilised Pullman stock that would otherwise have either been stabled on depots or used on non-Pullman workings. Trains were timed to leave London mid-morning and return in time for the stock to take up its scheduled evening working. Four such trains were operated:

1 The Chester Pullman
2 The West Country Pullman (Bath, Bristol, Exeter and Torbay)
3 The Stratford-upon-Avon Pullman (Oxford, Banbury, Leamington Spa, Warwick and Stratford-upon-Avon)
4 The Peak District Pullman (Derby, Chesterfield and Sheffield)

Only the first of these tourist trains was loco-hauled, the other three being part of HST diagrams. Poor marketing and a lack of imaginative destinations resulted in very poor patronage of this Pullman facility. The press latched on to the Stratford-upon-Avon Pullman in particular with the ensuing stories of 'ghost trains' run by BR!

SLEEPING CAR SERVICES

Sunday 15th May saw the last overnight sleeping car services operated on the East Coast route. From the following day all overnight Anglo–Scottish sleeping car trains used the capital's Euston station. This retrograde step 'cut off' many parts of Eastern England from overnight travel. On the positive side, the changes resulted in Birmingham gaining a sleeping car service to Aberdeen. A brand new service was introduced linking Poole, Bournemouth, Southampton and the Thames Valley with Glasgow and Edinburgh. The Scotland to Bristol service was extended to/from Plymouth. On summer Friday nights the sleeper was extended to Penzance to return from there on summer Saturdays.

Because of clearances on the Southern Region only stock fitted with short swing link bogies could be used on these services, and this resulted in a number of coach reallocations.

Sleeper Reception Cars (RLO) proved highly popular for first class passengers on Edinburgh–London services and were introduced on Glasgow–London service from May.

►Another of InterCity's new charges, Class 90 No. 90004 storms past MP142 at Slindon, North Staffordshire, 17th August. It is hauling the 14.30 Euston–Glasgow, the first regular service trains diagrammed for Class 90 haulage. *Hugh Ballantyne*

▼The May timetable saw the re-introduction of HST services to Liverpool Lime Street. On 16th May power car 43002 arrives at the head of the 06.16 ex-Bristol Temple Meads. *Doug Birmingham*

◀On an overcast 20th August, 43016 and 43033 arrive at Newquay prior to forming the 09.50 to Manchester Piccadilly. Newquay found a new importance in 1988 with all through trains to Paddington and the North being HSTs. The simple trackwork belies this importance, the terminus boasting just one siding. *Stephen Miller*

▼One of InterCity's short-formation trains designed to keep to HST schedules, the 08.18 Birmingham–Leeds seen at Ardsley, just short of its destination on 17th December 1988. Class 47 No. 47436 is at the helm. *Les Nixon*

◀The North East–South West main line produced a significant increase in the number of Class 31s working on summer Saturdays. Working in multiple, there were often up to three such workings each way every Saturday. Railfreight traction was diagrammed on these InterCity 'Holidaymaker' trains, one train being the 10.10 Manchester–Paignton seen at Dawlish on 11th June headed by Nos. 31206 and 31131. *Colin Marsden*

▲Following derailment of a freight train at Cupar on 2nd June and the resultant damage to track and a road bridge, the line from Dundee to Ladybank could not be used for some days and diversions took place over the single track from Hilton Junction to Ladybrook via Newburgh and Glenbirnie (which normally carries about three trains a day). Looking very out of place, the 07.55 'Flying Scotsman' from Aberdeen to King's Cross passes the old Glenbirnie Junction headed by power car No. 43056 'University of Bradford'.

Brian Morrison

►Through services between the north west and Kent were pruned from the May timetable due to poor patronage. Connections with feeder services were usually poor, timings were awkward for business travellers in particular, and major centres such as Birmingham were ill-served. One of the services removed from the start of 1988/9 timetable was the 09.04 Canterbury West–Liverpool Lime Street seen here passing Shoreham in Kent shortly after the start of its lengthy journey north. No. 47628 is in charge on 6th February.

Rodney Lissenden

▲The short-lived Class 37/4-hauled 15.30 (FO) Derby–St. Pancras and 18.20 (FO) return is seen here on the third weekend of duty, on 21st October. 37428 'David Lloyd George' waits to leave St. Pancras on its 128-mile run to Derby. *Brian Morrison*

▼Even in October 1988 it was still possible to find a 'Peak' on the Midland Main Line. 45106 waits for departure with its diagrammed service with the 17.50 to Derby on Friday 21st October. InterCity has agreed on this evening service and the 07.12 Derby–St. Pancras when not in 'special service'. When first repainted, the loco had the last three digits – its number painted on the front end in Railfreight manner. This, thankfully was removed later. *Brian Morrison*

▲1988 saw the new Class 90 Bo–Bo electrics enter service on the West Coast Main Line. Here 90004 is seen approaching Stafford on 7th September with the 14.30 Euston–Glasgow. *Hugh C. Betteridge*

▼The 'Stratford-on-Avon Pullman', in its first week of operation, the 10.40 Paddington–Stratford formed of an HST set headed by 43185 is seen ascending Hatton Bank on 17th May. *Chris Morrison*

▲**OLD AND NEW ON THE HOPE VALLEY. Class 31 No. 31437 heads a Liverpool–Sheffield train through Edale on 21st March with new Class 156 No. 156 404 (which had worked a press special) standing in the up siding.** *Les Nixon*

▼**After having had problems with railbuses, West Yorkshire PTE decided on a change of policy and took delivery of seven Class 155s to ease overcrowding. Here No. 155 342 in the PTE's cream and red livery is seen leaving Bradford Interchange with a Halifax–Leeds service on 20th November. Unfortunately for the PTE, all Class 155s were to be taken out of traffic with door problems by the end of the year.** *Les Nixon*

PROVINCIAL

Without doubt, the launch of the 'Express' network was the most important development of 1988. Other changes were as important for the long-term future of rural railways but received little coverage. For example, in October the Cambrian routes' radio signalling was commissioned. The RETB scheme meant that signalling staff requirements fell from 34 to 8, all based at the Machynlleth signalling centre. Also in Wales, new bridge construction was completed at Glanrhyd and a through Shrewsbury–Swansea service was re-introduced on 3rd October, twelve months after the collapse of the original bridge.

The continuing displacement of asbestos-lined stock continued. Almost completely a Provincial (and Network SouthEast) problem, it is a big task. At Plymouth Laira, the depot received the last Class 122 'bubble cars' following asbestos removal, which allowed replacement of some Class 118 asbestos-lined stock, including the well-known P460, the unit in the garish British Telecom advertising livery, which moved to Bristol.

Returning to the theme of a year of contracts we saw expansion and the threat of contraction of the network. Following the Railway Development Society's initial lobbying, the Nuneaton–Coventry trial service (started in 1987) was expanded into a full Sprinter-operated Nottingham–Coventry service from May.From one line's success, it was sad to hear Provincial management saying in November that they were looking at further cost savings on lightly-used lines - for which read possible closures as pruning for eventual 'privatisation'.

EXPRESS

At the beginning of the year Provincial was formulating its plan to show its new Class 155 and 156 'Super Sprinters' nationwide and to launch its exciting new network of 'Express' services. Early March saw presentations of the new rolling stock. The aim of 'Express' was to provide a frequent service over the 'core' section of routes (Manchester–Nottingham–Peterborough–Ely) with alternating origination and terminal points. Trains would normally be formed as two-car sets although some would operate as portion trains attaching or dctaching cn-routc. Most routcs on which thcsc new units would operate were in the hands of locomotive-hauled stock with motive power being provided by Class 31, 33 or 37 locomotives. Most loco-hauled trains were providing far more seats than a two-car 'Sprinter' could offer.

However, Provincial was confident that smaller, but more frequent and faster, in terms of overall journey times, trains would provide more, or at least an equivalent number of seats during the day. In theory this looked like a winner, but in practice it is virtually impossible to get passengers to change their travel habits. Therefore, whilst a fair amount of space was available on some trains, on others passengers had to stand or in some cases were unable to board the train, thus meaning they were forced to wait for the next service an hour later. Services operating to Blackpool or Norwich (for Yarmouth) during the summer months were particularly affected.

At the start of the summer timetable the new Windsor Link was opened in Manchester to allow operation of the 'Express' services between East Anglia and Blackpool. This important link was not due to be used by other services as well until May 1989.

Previously-sleepy Ely became a major interchange for Express services. £250,000 was spent upgrading facilities. Ely, rather than Peterborough, was chosen partly because of its wide, uncongested platforms.

The Western Region's 'Express' services, which utilise the fleet of 35 Leyland Bus-buiit Class 155 sets were not without problems. Once again overcrowding gave cause for concern with the result that Class 37/4 loco-hauled trains took over some Cardiff–Liverpool/Manchester and Cardiff–Taunton diagrams. This in turn released three Class 155 sets to strengthen Cardiff–Portsmouth trains.

Door control defects on the Class 155s have also caused British Rail a major headache and on occasions availability has been very low. On 16th December, following the opening of a passenger door whilst a 155 was in motion, the decision was taken to take the entire fleet out of service. As a contingency measure the Class 156 units at Haymarket and Inverness depots, in readiness for the ScotRail launch in early 1989, were immediately moved south. After 3 days' improvising using Class 33-hauled trains, SR DEMUs and WR DMUs, the key Cardiff–Portsmouth route was able to offer a Class 156-operated service.

In the North East Class 156 units took over Newcastle–Carlisle–Stranraer/Girvan services from 3rd October. Between Newcastle and Carlisle the service was previously in the hands of a mixture of conventional DMUs and Class 143 'Pacer' units.

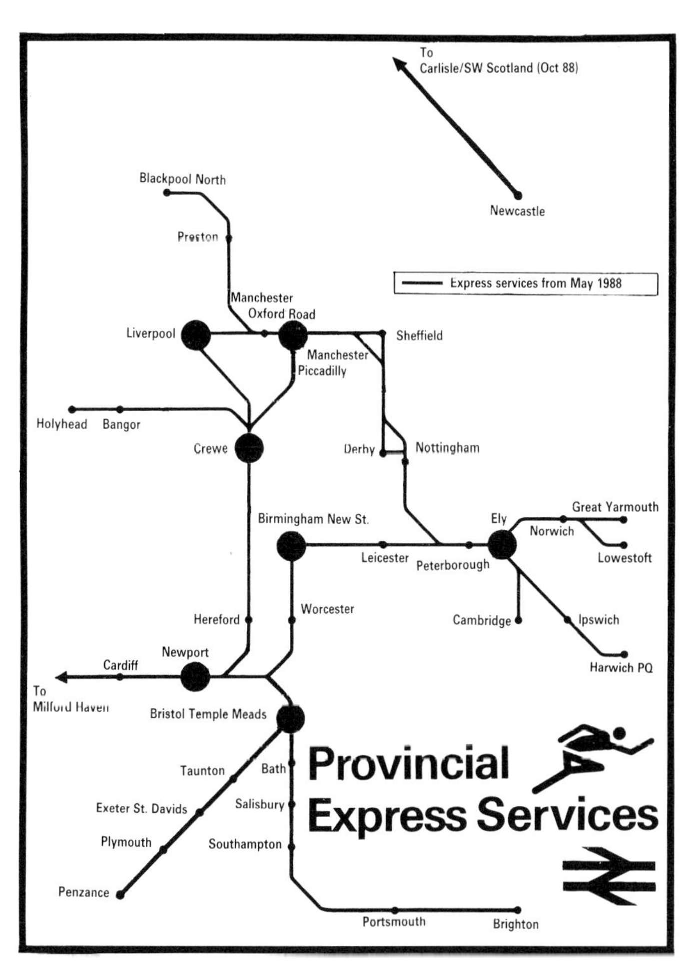

▲Provincial's Express network is a bold attempt to further improve the sector's performance by dramatically improving – in terms of greater passenger comfort and reduced journey times – the service offered to passengers. The superior acceleration of Sprinters did indeed result in welcome journey time reductions.

◄►Regional press launches of Provincial's Express network took place at Manchester, Nottingham, Ely, Ledbury and Weston-Super-Mare. Sheffield was host to a 'publicity stunt' with Bernie Clifton making an appearance. Does Provincial's Sprinter symbol represent a passenger running for his connection that is not being held?!
Peter Fox

◄Brand new Class 156 No. 156 420 passes Wymondham on the 07.30 Liverpool–Norwich Provincial Express service. At 10 miles south west of Norwich, Wymondham looked a shadow of its former self for many years. David Turner, a local businessman and railway enthusiast took over the listed buildings in 1988 and tastefully refurbished them into a chandelier-lit showroom and is working on 'Brief Encounter' tea rooms. In this view, on 24th August, the station already looks more cared-for. Just behind the Sprinter is the start of the Wymondham–North Elmham branch; during 1988 the Wymondham and Dereham Action Committee continued to press for a restoration of through passenger trains from Dereham to Norwich. *Steve Turner*

◄From 16th May 1988, all Class 33-hauled trains were replaced by Class 155 Super Sprinters on Portsmouth–Bristol–Cardiff workings. There were many complaints of overcrowding, most trains consisting of 2 rather than 5 coaches as before. In addition to the 'core' service there were useful extensions to the new service, for example, a Class 155-operated Milford Haven–Brighton return service. On the evening of 14th June unit 155 305 leaves Westbury with the 18.10 Portsmouth–Cardiff. On the left 155 301 and 155 305 wait with the 18.19 Cardiff–Portsmouth service. *G.F. Gillham*

►Whilst Provincial improved the standard of long-distance travel over some of its routes, the holidaymaker was often made to suffer. The 08.55 Manchester Piccadilly–Great Yarmouth was diagrammed for a 2 x 3-car Class 108 DMUs from Buxton depot. However, the DMUs were later commandeered for Sheffield–Blackpool relief workings with the Manchester Yarmouth train becoming loco hauled. This photograph shows sets BX379 (51948/59389/52050) and BX376 (52064/59388/51941) passing through the Fenland village of Chettisham on 21st May, the first Saturday of operation.
Michael J. Collins

►The Windsor Link was intended to overcome some of the shortcomings of the original rail network in Manchester, notably a lack of connection between southern-orientated routes (based on Piccadilly) and northern-orientated routes (based on Victoria). Class 156 No. 156 404, the unit used for regional press launches of Express services, traverses the Windsor Link on 13th August with the 11.16 Cambridge–Blackpool service. *Les Nixon*

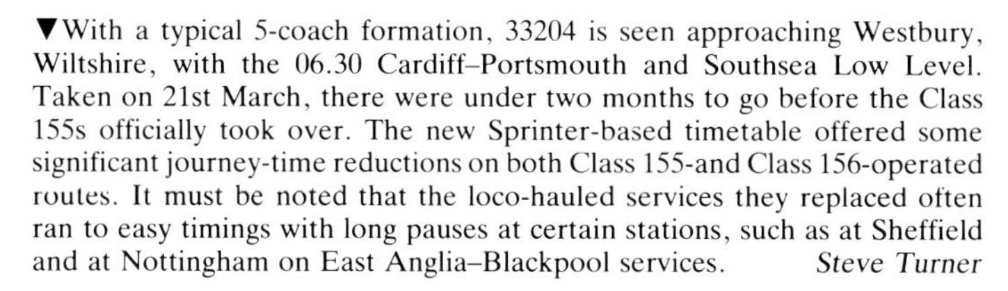

▼With a typical 5-coach formation, 33204 is seen approaching Westbury, Wiltshire, with the 06.30 Cardiff–Portsmouth and Southsea Low Level. Taken on 21st March, there were under two months to go before the Class 155s officially took over. The new Sprinter-based timetable offered some significant journey-time reductions on both Class 155-and Class 156-operated routes. It must be noted that the loco-hauled services they replaced often ran to easy timings with long pauses at certain stations, such as at Sheffield and at Nottingham on East Anglia–Blackpool services. *Steve Turner*

◄Due to shortages of new Class 156 Sprinter units, certain East Anglian services were diagrammed for Class 150s pending delivery of more 156s. Here, No. 150 150 passes Ely North Junction with a Cambridge–Birmingham New Street service on 3rd June 1988. *Michael J. Collins*

▼Diagrammed to cover for non-availability of Class 150/1 Sprinters, Class 45 No. 45128 hauls the 16.22 Leeds–Nottingham along the Holmes Chord, Rotherham, opened to traffic in 1987. 'Peaks', Class 31s and Class 47s all appeared on this service. Passengers were, no doubt, grateful for the extra seating capacity on this service, as it was usually 'full and standing' leaving Sheffield. The date is 15th March. *Les Nixon*

◄With unreliable Class 143 units from Heaton, many trains between Newcastle and Carlisle, Newcastle and Middlesbrough and Newcastle and Berwick-upon-Tweed were loco-hauled. Class 47s, 31s and even some 45s appeared as substitutes. Thornaby-based Class 31 No. 31283 is at Carlisle on the 26th August on the 18.55 Carlisle–Newcastle service. *Paul Gash*

METROPOLITAN AREAS

Manchester, Merseyside, Tyne and Wear and the Yorkshire PTEs voiced concern during the year at the poor reliability and availability of the 'pacer' fleet operating on their section 20-supported services. British Rail took note of the complaints and instigated a modification programme to replace the self-changing gears transmission system with one of Voith manufacture on its own units. BR did not alter the PTE-owned units' transmissions and by the year's end some PTEs were threatening legal action against BR.

Ordered as an attempt to relieve overcrowding, West Yorkshire PTE took delivery of its 10 centre powered cars which have been used to strengthen 10 Class 144 'Pacer' sets to 3-car units. These units were diagrammed for use on local routes but the PTE had to make representations to BR after some sets were noted working in South Yorkshire and elsewhere.

West Yorkshire also took delivery of seven Class 155 'Super-Sprinter' units for use on the 'Calder Valley' line. These units were purchased outright in a contract between the PTE and Leyland Bus, without remit to the standard British Rail tendering and procurement procedure.

In South Yorkshire new stations at Goldthorpe and Thurnscoe were opened in May and are served by infrequent Sheffield–York services as well as the new hourly Sprinter service between Sheffield and Leeds via the Dearne Valley. At the same time the PTE commenced support, under the section 20 agreement, for Bolton-on-Dearne station. Support for the Sheffield–Barnsley–Huddersfield service was extended from Penistone to be contiguous with the South Yorkshire/West Yorkshire boundary. This eliminated British Rail support for the service from 16th May. The agreement also provided the Sheffield–Huddersfield line with a Sunday service during summer months. The first Sunday service on the line for many years.

In the Birmingham area services were improved on 28th November when trains were extended from City station to a re-opened Trent Valley high level station in Lichfield.

In May, Bedworth station was re-opened, between Coventry and Nuneaton, and became served by a new hourly Coventry–Nottingham service.

Delays by the PTE in adopting a new livery resulted in facelifted Class 310 units emerging from works painted in standard Provincial services livery.

In Glasgow, the Strathclyde PTE-sponsored Coatbridge Central–Hamilton–Dalmuir services continued to operate after their successful trial period in 1987

▲► With five coaches in tow on a Class 155 diagram, Class 37/4 No. 37428 David Lloyd George rounds the curve at Marsh Brook with the 13.17 Liverpool–Cardiff service on 7th October. These regular loco-hauled Sprinter substitutes were due to cease on 1st October but some trains were still being loco-hauled by year's end. *Geoff Bannister*

► Some Class 144 Pacers were strengthened to 3 car units, being ordered by West Yorkshire PTE. A Scunthorpe–Leeds service stands adjacent to a Leeds–Scunthorpe service in the bay platforms at Doncaster on 9th July. WYPTE were not very pleased to discover that their new vehicles were being used beyond their boundaries.
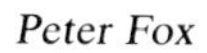
Peter Fox

CROSS-COUNTRY BOAT TRAINS

In Volume 1 of 'Today's Railways Review of the Year' it was reported that the 'European' (Glasgow/Edinburgh–Harwich PQ), operated by the InterCity sector had been re-routed via North London in May 1987. The savings of 78 minutes on the end-to-end journey time was far outweighed by the reduction in passengers who now used the service. The main passenger corridor through Manchester–Sheffield, Nottingham and Peterborough was now lost to Crewe, Birmingham, Watford. Quite often the train was virtually empty upon leaving Birmingham on the southbound service. Publicity for the 'European' was very sparse and it was especially difficult to find in the public timetable, which certainly contributed to its low patronage, a fact reported in in depth on a BBC TV 'That's Life' programme early in the year. The 'European' was withdrawn in May 1988.

The 'European' had been replaced by 'The Rheinlander', a seven-coach second class-only service between Harwich PQ and Manchester Piccadilly. This in turn was replaced with the start of the new summer 1988 timetable by 'The Loreley', between Harwich PQ and Blackpool formed of one 2-car Class 156. As predicted, this service was grossly overcrowded at busy times, particularly between Sheffield and Blackpool, and to a lesser extent between Nottingham and Sheffield. It was not until the winter that 'The Loreley' was generally strengthened; even over the Christmas period overcrowded 2-car trains were operated on certain days.

The other problem was that of the trains connecting with the boat. 'The Loreley' leaflet advertising the services refers to the train services as 'connections'. But when is a connection not a connection? Apparently when the boat is late! The following story illustrates the lack of commitment of BR Provincial to the 'Boat Train' concept.

On 13th August, the publisher's daughter, returning with heavy luggage from a work-period in the Netherlands, caught the day boat from Hoek van Holland to Harwich, having chosen this route purely because of the direct connection to Sheffield. She arrived at Harwich Parkeston Quay station at 18.35 due to a delay in disembarkation from the ship. The 18.25 to Manchester Oxford Road had already departed.

As a result she was forced to travel to Sheffield via London, an arduous journey that involved having to sit in the vestibule of the packed London-bound train and carrying four heavy bags (one of which the 16-stone publisher could hardly lift) when travelling by Underground to St. Pancras. The whole journey took 1¼ hours longer than planned.

Mr A.Shingler, Marketing Manager, Express and Anglia Services replied to the ensuing letter of complaint: "As you quite rightly state in your letter the 18.25 from Harwich is shown in the Loreley leaflet as connecting out of the Hoek van Holland–Harwich Parkeston Quay sailing. However I must advise you that this cannot be taken as a guarantee that the service will be held in the event of late running of the boat". He points out that continental traffic passengers are outnumbered by domestic passengers who also might have important connections, for instance at Peterborough.

Clearly, when incoming boat (or train) services are running late, there is always a conflict of interest between the needs of the incoming passengers who do not want to be delayed. But to advertise a through boat–train connecting service and then not to hold the train for a few minutes is surely unacceptable, especially as the alternative offered – crossing London – is no substitute for a through service, particularly for passengers travelling with heavy luggage. Perhaps the worst part of the story is that the BR letter replying to the complaint held up no hope for the future and ended "... I would suggest that in this instance your complaint should have been directed to them [Sealink] as the failure was on their part not ours"!

Manchester Piccadilly
Ipswich—Stowmarket—Bury St. Edmunds—Ely—March—Peterborough—Grantham—Nottingham—Alfreton & Mansfield Parkway—Chesterfield—Sheffield—Stockport

▲The 'Rheinlander' window sticker.

◀The last westbound 'Rheinlander', on 14th May, passes the former Millhouses motive power depot between Dore and Sheffield, with Class 47/4 No. 47585 *County of Cambridgeshire* hauling a rake of air-braked Mark 2A/B/C stock. *Peter Fox*

▼The last timetabled westbound working of an InterCity train over the 'European's route was the 13.30 Harwich Parkeston Quay–Birmingham on Sunday 15th May seen passing Homerton with 86232 *Harold Macmillan* in charge. *Michael McGowan*

THE LORELEY.

Overcrowding was a particular problem on the 'Loreley', the 07.57 Harwich Parkeston Quay–Blackpool North, a two-car unit proving inadequate on many occasions.

▲Passengers struggle to board the 'Loreley' at Sheffield Midland on Saturday 21st May, but many are unlucky. *Peter Fox*

▲►Some of the 'lucky' passengers who managed to squeeze in. *Peter Fox*

►Even as late as 28th December the train was not always strengthened and, as might be expected over the holiday period, overcrowding was still occurring. *Mick King*

▼The real 'Loreley' heads south through Koblenz, West Germany on 9th June formed of 110 151-8 and a mixture of DB & SBB coaching stock. *Peter Fox*

▲BR provided the Conwy Valley's Sunday trains in 1988, with support from Gwynedd County Council. They did not carry the usual 'Sunday Shuttles' headboard. The North Wales Railway Circle provided excellent commentary on the history and scenic delights of the line on the Tyseley Class 117 seen here when the new season of service commenced on 17th July. Right Lines Catering provided refreshments. *Larry Goddard*

◀Thirty years old, but given a reprieve (involving asbestos removal), that will see it in operation for years to come, Class 122 single power car No. 55000, numerically the first of the batch, runs through Luxulyan on 31st March with the 12.05 Par–Newquay service. At the end of the year the two Class 122 units allocated to Network SouthEast at Bletchley were transferred to Laira for use on Provincial's Devon and Cornwall services. *Les Nixon*

▼Tyseley four-car suburban unit T418 comprising 53116, 59611, 59643 and 51880 forms 10.22 Birmingham New Street–Lichfield Trent Valley service, conveying civic dignitaries, on 28th November. The banner proclaims the extension to the cross-city line from the same day with almost all Lichfield trains using the re-opened Lichfield Trent Valley High Level station (for connections to West Coast Main Line services). The re-opening ceremony also involved the now-mandatory cracking of detonators and screaming children.! *Steven Knight*

NETWORK SOUTHEAST

With three electrification schemes completed, an important new cross-London route opened, and with three new and modern types of electric multiple unit entering service, 1988 was an eventful and significant year for Network SouthEast. In 'Thameslink', the Capital now has a line comparable with the much-vaunted 'RER' in Paris, while the new Class 442 'Wessex Electric' units have for the first time brought Mark 3 standards of accommodation to travellers on Network SouthEast's premier route.

Among smaller projects completed during 1988, new stations have been built at Arlesley, Martins Heron and How Wood, while rebuilding, refurbishment or even just plain repainting has been taking place at many other locations. The Network SouthEast image is now being seen on the more remote parts of the Network, the Bedford–Bletchley line being a notable example.

Of the new projects announced during the year, the most important is probably the electrification of the Portsmouth Harbour–Eastleigh/Southampton 'Hantsway' link, which will enable many more through journey and diversionary opportunities for electric stock. Resignalling is taking place on the Oxted–Uckfield and Strood–Maidstone West lines. Twenty four new Class 456 two-car EMUs have been ordered, for use on the South West subsector.

Much of the above has, however, been overshadowed by the appalling carnage of the Clapham Junction disaster, in which 35 persons lost their lives. Similarly, the murder of a 26-year-old woman in a closed compartment of a train of 'EPB' stock in March served to draw media attention and public concern to the subject of the personal safety of railway passengers in a most unfortunate way. Other problems faced during the year included an acute shortage of staff, particularly on the South Central subsector, resulting in the removal of many trains from the peak-hour timetable from July and intermittent cancellation of other services on a seemingly random basis. Late delivery of new stock from BREL (1988) Ltd and seemingly poor quality control has caused difficulties for operating staff and depots, and continuing rebuilding at Liverpool Street and Victoria stations has caused often unnecessary chaos for many thousands of commuters and resultant bad public relations.

▲Work going on: A major and much- needed reconstruction has been taking place at Guildford, formerly one of the tattiest major stations on Network SouthEast. Most of the platform awnings have been flattened in this view, looking north, photographed on 13th October. On platform 5, a Waterloo-bound train waits to depart. *Kevin Lane*

►Work completed: A most pleasing refurbishment of the station building at Aylesford, on the rural Strood–Maidstone West–Paddock Wood line in Kent, was completed during 1988. On 6th December, Class 411/5 '4 Cep' EMU 1593 pulls in with the 11.53 Paddock Wood–Strood service. The unit is in the now-obsolescent two-tone brown 'jaffa cake' livery, while the impressive semaphore signal on the left will soon be swept away as part of a recently-announced resignalling scheme for the line. *Brian Morrison*

DEVELOPING THE NETWORK IMAGE

Following experimental application to SR Class 423 EMU 3150 in 1987, there were changes to the Network SouthEast livery applied to rolling stock from the start of 1988. A darker shade of blue was introduced as being 'kinder to the countryside', while the upsweeps at the cab ends of units were given a curve rather than a sharp angle. There have been subtle alterations to the thickness of the red lines on various batches of stock, particularly at cab ends and along cantrails, while on new Class 321 and 442 EMUs, the dark grey has been replaced by a much lighter shade, on the 442s covering the roof as well.

A retrograde step, particularly for enthusiasts but also for depot staff, was the repositioning of unit numbers on the front ends of SR corridor units and DEMUs. Initially, numbers were moved from their traditional position above the cab windows to a lower position below them, but on the drivers side only, where on 'Vep'/'Cig'/'TC'-type stock it was all but hidden by a handrail! It was soon repeated on both sides, but still looked awful. Late in the year, however, common sense prevailed, and unit numbers returned to their traditional place.

▲Towards the end of the year, the '4 Cep' EMUs began to receive Network livery in place of the old 'jaffa cake' scheme. Among the first to be so repainted were 1560 and 1561, and ususually both can be seen in this view of Paddock Wood, photographed on 10th December. On the left, 1560 passes through non-stop leading the 10.56 Charing Cross–Dover–Ramsgate service, while in the right background 1561 calls with the 11.00 from Charing Cross to Ashford. On this front end, the unit numbers have remained in their traditional position, there really being nowhere else to put them. *Alex Dasi-Sutton*

◀Network SouthEast livery also spread to the Class 101 and 119 DMUs used on Reading to Gatwick Airport/Tonbridge services during 1988. The only unit of the former type on this route so far thus painted, L835 (vehicles 51498, 59530 and 51432), calls at Reigate with the 10.40 Reading–Gatwick Airport on the last day of 1988. *Alex Dasi-Sutton*

▼During 1988, several routes on Network SouthEast were given 'line names', and where stock is solely allocated to a particular route, transfer badges have been applied, generally on the blank area next to the doors on sliding door stock. Similar badges are being applied to new stock working only in a particular area. Although the idea is good in that it gives each particular route its own identity, some of the names chosen show a distinct lack of imagination, especially as the names chosen were often the winning result of a competition! Shown from the left are: 'Harlequin Line' (Euston– Watford stopping service, an amalgam of several station names on the route, carried on appropriate Class 313s); 'Great Northern Line' (suburban and outer-suburban services out of King's Cross, carried by appropriate 313s and 317s); and 'Wessex Electrics' (carried by 442s working the Waterloo–Weymouth route). Other names include the really original (!?) 'Northampton Line' (What is wrong with 'Cobblers Line' we ask?), 'Anglia Electrics' and, of course, 'Thameslink'. *All: Brian Morrison*

INAUGURATION OF THAMESLINK

Undoubtedly the most important development on Network SouthEast during 1988 was the inauguration of Thameslink. This involved the reopening, following relaying and electrification on the SR 750 V dc system, of the former LCDR 'Metropolitan Extension' from Blackfriars to the Bedford–Moorgate route at Farringdon, allowing through running from the Bedford line to Southern Region destinations. Commencing on 16th May, the main service operates from Bedford to Gatwick Airport or Brighton. Off-peak, trains work from Cricklewood to Orpington and Sevenoaks via the Catford loop, and from Luton to Purley alternately via Crystal Palace and via Selhurst. This gives a total of six trains an hour in each direction from Blackfriars through the tunnel to King's Cross Thameslink (the former Midland City station in Pentonville Road). During the peaks, a number of trains loop round from Streatham to Sutton and back.

The first of the new Class 319 electric units for this service were already working on the Bedford–St Pancras/Moorgate line at the start of the year, displacing 317s, but as further units were delivered from York Works, trial running began on the Southern from January, with regular mileage accumulation runs down the Brighton line from 1st March. Weekend trips in passenger service on the Brighton line ran from 9th April, the first being in a snowstorm! On 26th April, 319 031 and 319 033 made record time on special runs from London Bridge to Brighton and return to Victoria. An unadvertised off-peak Gatwick Airport to Luton service commenced from 28th April, but these trips were frequently cancelled due to staff shortage.

With barely two-thirds off the 60-strong Class 319 fleet delivered and working by May, it was something of a gamble to start the complete new service. Several peak trains were formed of four cars only, leading to justified complaints of

◀Negotiating the reopened section of line from Blackfriars which enables Thameslink services to operate, 319 039 approaches Farringdon Junction with a Luton-bound service on 25th May. The line going off to the left continues to Moorgate, now only served by Thameslink trains in the peaks. *Ian Cowley*

▼Prior to the start of Thameslink services, route learning trips were operated on the lines to be served, making use of both WR DMUs and route learning saloons propelled by Class 33 or 73 locomotives. On 10th May, Gloucester Class 119 diesel unit L576 is a most unusual sight at Blackfriars, forming the 13.15 route learning trip from Purley. *Rodney Lissenden*

▲319 044, in the later dark blue Network SouthEast livery applied to 319 026 upwards, arrives at Farringdon with the 16.52 Luton–Sutton service on 4th August, no doubt much to the relief of waiting commuters. Here, the pantograph will come down as the unit changes from working off 25 kV ac overhead to the SR 750 V dc third-rail system. *Chris Wilson*

▼Working 'under the wires', 319 020 approaches Luton with a late-running stopping service from Purley. The unit number is repeated under each cab window of the 'B' DTSO to denote to platform staff the coach with the 'convertible' parcels saloon behind the driver's cab, which can be locked off when in use. The other end of the unit has only a single number on the driver's side. *Alex Dasi-Sutton*

▶The main Thameslink service operates half-hourly between Bedford and Gatwick Airport, alternate trains continuing to Brighton. On 6th June, 319 010 commences its long trek from the South Coast, passing Lovers Walk Depot (Brighton) with the 14.30 to Bedford. The 319s are standard class only, causing grumbles from first class season ticket holders on the Brighton line, particularly in rush hours. From October, the rear vehicle of the 06.10 from Brighton was reserved for such passengers using window stickers, but the cramped 3+2 seating is no match for a first class compartment in a 'Cig'!
David Brown

overcrowding. There were problems with the new units, particularly with the doors, GTO thyristor control equipment, and pantographs raising on the SR third rail sections and hitting bridges! However, these problems have now been overcome, largely due to sterling efforts by staff at Selhurst Depot (where the 319s are maintained) and they are now among the more reliable EMUs in the Network SouthEast fleet. With deliveries completed by October, many 4-car trains were made up to 8 cars from the start of the winter timetable. Network SouthEast are very pleased with the success of Thameslink in its first summer of operation, and twenty more Class 319s have been ordered to augment services.

THE 'WESSEX ELECTRICS' ARRIVE

May 1988 saw the completion of the Branksome (Bournemouth) to Weymouth electrification scheme, and a completely recast timetable came into effect from the start of the new timetable. However, due to the very late delivery of the new Class 442 'Wessex Electric' EMUs for the route, some interim arrangements were necessary.

The new timetable is based around an hourly fast service, calling at Southampton Parkway, Southampton, Brockenhurst, Bournemouth, Poole, Wareham and all stations to Weymouth; there is also an hourly semifast to Poole, and hourly Waterloo–Southampton and Southampton–Wareham stopping trains, with a corresponding service in the up direction. Due to the late delivery of the new Class 442 'Wessex Electrics' with their 100 mph capability, however, the timetable had to be modified to make use of existing rolling stock resources. This mainly involved starting and terminating the fasts at Bournemouth, with a connecting shuttle through to Weymouth, formed of a refurbished 'Vep'.

From 16th May, only five Class 442 units were available for service, and these were concentrated on peak-hour workings as far as possible. As more entered service, through Saturday workings to Weymouth started from 16th July. By the end of the year, units up to 2422 were in traffic, in spite of promises made that all would be in service by October!

▲A new face at Weymouth. Class 442 EMU 2413 stands in Platform 2 of the much rebuilt and rationalised Weymouth station, waiting to depart with the 12.53 to Waterloo on Saturday 15th October. *Alex Dasi-Sutton*

▲Class 442 units from 2413 were built with a bar lounge area replacing part of the luggage space in the centre Motor Buffet Luggage Standard, and earlier units are being modified to conform. This view shows 62957 from unit 2421 at Wareham on 30th December. The new lounge is situated behind the two small windows. Also shown clearly are the power-operated swing plug doors, fitted (not entirely successfully) to Mark 3 stock for the first time in mainland Britain. *Chris Wilson*

◄One of the major projects of the Weymouth electrification scheme was the rebuilding of Poole station, where the new station building was only opened, still incomplete, in November. This unusual structure, together with the large new car park and station forecourt, are seen in this view taken on 30th December. 73138 'Post Haste' and 73112 prepare to depart with the 12.46 semi-fast service to Waterloo. *Chris Wilson*

▼The shape of things to come on the Bournemouth line, the new Class 442 'Wessex Electrics' units were first shown to the local press and public at Bournemouth Depot open day held on 26th March. Inside the new inspection shed prior to the start of the open day is 2403, bereft of NSE 'flashes' on the gangway ends. The appearance of the ends of these units coupled with the extensive use of plastic in their construction led to their gaining the nickname 'plastic pigs', although we understand that this was frowned upon by BR management. 2403 was later hauled out of the shed and pushed back in to the accompaniment of '2001' and much white smoke for the official unveiling. *Chris Wilson*

◄On Sunday 30th November, track relaying north of Winchester caused all Bournemouth/Weymouth line services to be diverted via Andover and Laverstock Junction (Salisbury). This brought the first visits of Class 442 units to this route, albeit diesel-hauled.It was soon found that Class 33/1 locomotives could not work with these units in the push/ pull mode (although their specification stated that they were supposed to be able to!), and thus all trains had to be hauled. Here, 33117 heads 2416 through Dean, forming the 09.02 Weymouth–Waterloo. *G F Gillham*

OTHER ELECTRIFICATION SCHEMES COMPLETED

▲The Watford Junction–St Albans Abbey branch was electrified as from 11th July, and a new station at How Wood was opened on the line from the start of the October timetable. The service is operated by Class 313 dual-voltage EMUs which also work the Euston–Watford Junction stopping services. On 28th August, 313 005 was pictured underneath the giant lighting stalks at St Albans Abbey waiting to depart with the 17.22 to Watford. *Paul Shannon*

▲Electrification from Royston to Cambridge was also completed during 1988, through King's Cross–Cambridge electric services starting from 16th May. Prior to the commencement of the full electric services, a special timetable was operated on Bank Holiday Monday 2nd May. Sporting an appropriate headboard, 317 338 arrives at Shepreth on that day with the 14.32 Cambridge–Royston 'shuttle'.
David Percival

►Royston–Cambridge electrification brought an end to this scene. Before the timetable change and on a miserable-looking 16th January,passengers make their way from the 12.05 King's Cross–Royston to the 13.00 Royston–Cambridge. The former has been operated by 317 352, the latter about to be operated by a Class 101 DMU, No.51438 being closest the camera (with 54382 leading).
David Percival

NEW CLASS 321 UNITS FOR ANGLIA REGION

The third new type of EMU to enter service since the formation of Network SouthEast, the Class 321 units are mainly for use on Anglia Region services from Liverpool Street to Cambridge and Southend Victoria. The new trains are basically a 25 kV only version of the Thameslink Class 319s, being based on the Mark 3 suburban sliding-door bodyshell, but incorporate several differences and refinements. These include Brush rather than GEC traction equipment, a small first class section in one of the driving trailers, and yet another new front end. Without any form of gangway or emergency exit, this latter is a very questionable improvement from the safety and security angle. Forty-six are being built initially, and the first to be completed was ceremoniously 'handed over' at BREL (1988) York Works on 15th September. A further 20 units have now been authorised (although NSE would have liked more) and a few will join Class 317s on services out of Euston.

▼The first 321s entered service on routes out of Liverpool Street as the year came to an end, just meriting a mention in this book. On 28th December, 321 307 passes Bethnal Green with the 11.25 from Cambridge. Points to note include the dot-matrix destination display and the 'P' suffix to the unit number – this denotes to platform staff the driving trailer with the convertible parcels area behind the cab. Livery includes the very light shade of grey first seen on the 'Wessex Electrics'. The front end is certainly stylish, showing a little French influence perhaps? *Brian Morrison*

CASCADES

▼The introduction of Class 319 'Thameslink' units onto the Midland suburban line enabled the Class 317 units formerly operating the 'Bedpan' route to be transferred to other Network SouthEast services. Some joined similar units working out of King's Cross, and the remainder were re-allocated to Bletchley, for use on outer suburban trains from Euston. Due to late delivery of 319s, however, some had to remain in use on peak-hour Bedford–St Pancras/Moorgate trains until the start of the October timetable. On 2nd June 317 313 is seen standing under Barlow's impressive single-span roof at St Pancras. *Les Nixon*

▼The Class 312 units formerly in use out of King's Cross were cascaded to Anglia Region services, together with their similar Class 310 sisters from the Euston lines. The last remaining pair of 312s allocated to Hornsey (the GN suburban depot), lead by 312 720, pass Haringay on 25th May, forming the 17.25 Kings Cross–Peterborough commuter service. *Ian Cowley*

▲1988 saw the opening of 'Thameslink', the brandname given to the service through the re-opened Snow Hill Tunnel in London. New dual-voltage EMUs of Class 319 were provided to operate the service which became an overnight success. This photograph taken at Farringdon shows 319 032 en route to Bedford and 319 050 heading for Three Bridges. *Gavin Morrison*

►Electrification from Bournemouth to Weymouth should have been accompanied by a changeover to new rolling stock, but late delivery meant that the new service started with most trains formed of old stock. 73119 *Kentish Mercury* and 73135 approach Pirbright on 25th June with the 11.47 Poole–Waterloo formed of TC stock, the first five coaches being a '5 TCB', a makeshift set cobbled up from a 4 TC and an ex-REP buffet car. *John Chalcraft*

▼The new Class 442 'Wessex Electric' stock was phased in gradually throughout the year. Nos. 2413 and 2414 are seen leaving Brockenhurst with the 08.48 Bournemouth–Waterloo on 6th August. These were the first two units to have a lounge area and reduced luggage space in the buffet vehicle. *G. F. Gillham*

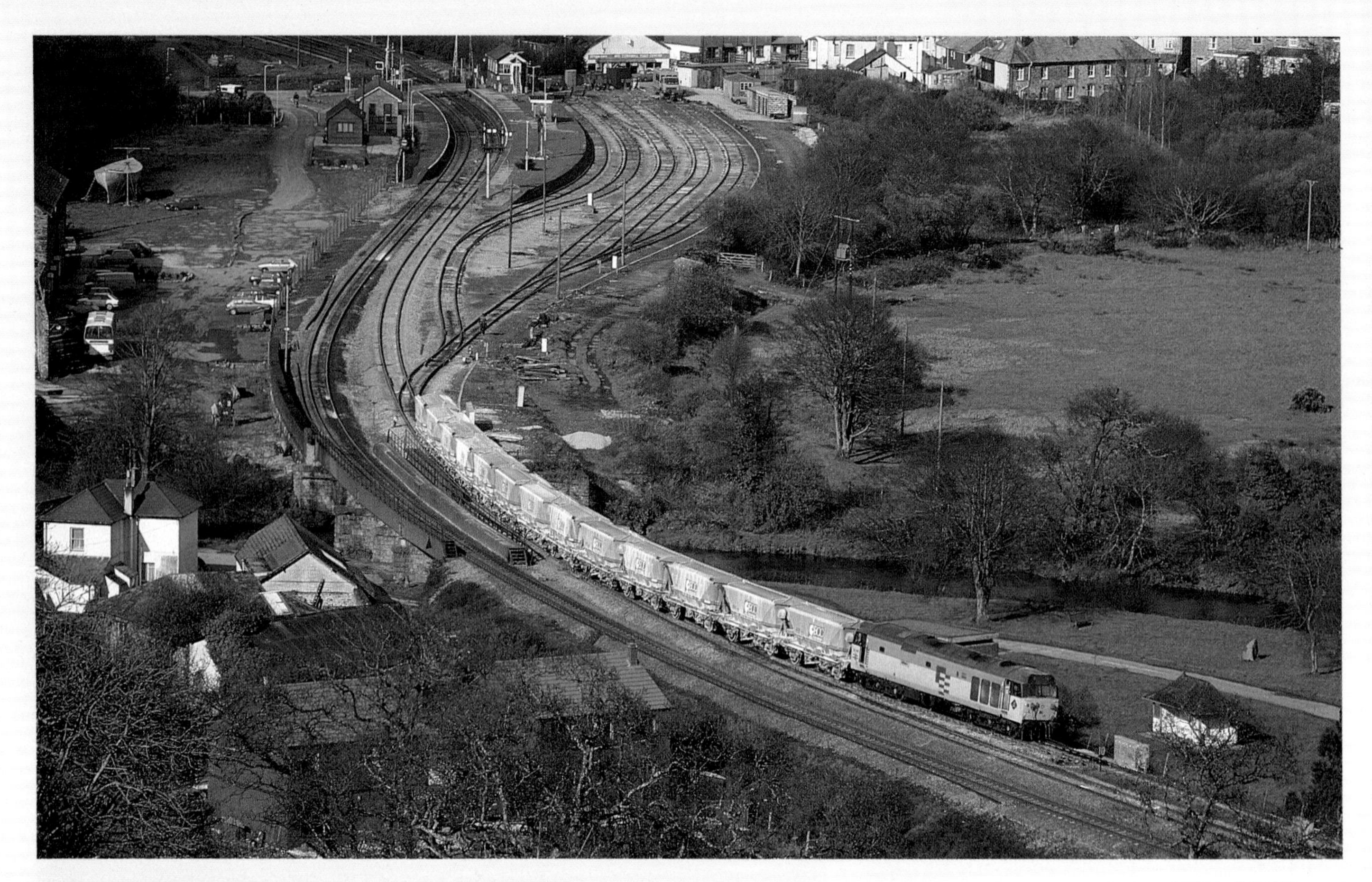

▲Railfreight's unsuccessful Class 50 conversion, No. 50149 *Defiance*, spent much of 1988 employed on local china clay duties in Cornwall. On 25th April No. 50149 draws to a halt in the down loop at Par with empty CDAs from Fowey. The train was divided here, the first 16 wagons being taken on to Burngullow while the remainder were collected later from St. Blazey *G. F. Gillham*

◀ A major innovation in wagon design for 1988 was the Redland self-discharge train, allowing deliveries to be made to terminals with no specialist facilities. A regular service from Mountsorrel to Langley Junction, just south of Stevenage, commenced in May. The 09.05 Langley Junction–Mountsorrel working is pictured heading north from Welwyn Garden City on 23rd August, having run-round in the up sidings there. *Paul Shannon*

▶ Nos. 33208 and 33211 leave Dover with a minestone train from Snowdown Colliery to Sevington on the afternoon of 1st September. The sidings at Snowdown had been specially reinstated for this traffic. The minestone is carried in purpose-made PXA box wagons built on the underframes of redundant Shell oil tankers. Also of interest is the inclusion of a brake van in the train, needed for shunting manouvres at Ashford.
Alex Dasi-Sutton

RAILFREIGHT

Railfreight is now well-established as a self-supporting and profitable branch of BR operations. Railfreight's income for the financial year 1987–8 was a healthy £555 m., whilst the operating surplus of £43.6 m. for the same period was the highest for over a decade. The key to this success has been the continuing quest for greater efficiency, with resources of every kind trimmed to whatever level can be justified by traffic levels. Whilst locomotive and wagon fleets continue to shrink, the tonnage of freight carried on BR remains roughly constant, with new profitable freight flows taking the place of those which have been discarded on economic grounds.

Readers will by now be familiar with the policy of sub-sector dedication of resources, or 'sectorisation' as it is commonly known. By the end of 1988 almost all BR's locomotive fleet had been allotted to specific pools, following the example set by North Thameside petroleum traffic and one or two other pilot schemes. It has always been common practice for main line passenger locomotives to stray long distances from their home depot, but the concentration of freight traction at a few strategic depots, each covering large areas of the network, is relatively new. Perhaps the most striking example of this policy is the Speedlink locomotive fleet, most of which is based at Tinsley. At the end of 1988 the Tinsley fleet comprised 101 Class 47s, 34 Class 37s and 29 Class 31s. Between them these locomotives cover almost all trunk and feeder services on the network, stretching as far as Exeter, Dover, Holyhead and Mossend. The only main line Speedlink locomotives not based at Tinsley are the West Coast main line electrics and some lower-powered traction for feeder services, mainly on the Southern and Scottish regions.

Other examples of dedicated locomotive fleets are Class 20s for the North West coal, Class 31s for nuclear flask traffic, Class 37/0s for the Speedlink Coal network, Class 37/5s for Teesside steel, Cornish china clay and Buxton stone, Class 37/7s for North Thameside oil, Class 37/7s and 37/9s for South Wales steel, Class 47s for Stanlow oil, Class 56s for WR and LMR aggregates, Class 56s for trainload coal in the Midlands and North East, and Class 58s for East Midlands coal. There are still occasions when one sub-sector uses traction borrowed from another sub-sector, just as Railfreight traction is sometimes diagrammed for seasonal passenger workings, but such occasions are kept to a minimum. Oddities such as the use of Class 58 on Freightliner workings south of Birmingham have now largely been eliminated. The use of dedicated locomotive fleets has made it easier for the lineside observer to identify freight workings: if a trans-Pennine oil train is hauled by a Crewe Class 47, it is more likely to be travelling to/from Stanlow than to/from Immingham or Port Clarence!

Railfreight's core traffics are represented by the sub sectors Coal, Construction, Petroleum and Metals, and all of these produced good results in 1988. A particular growth area for Construction was stone from the Mendips and Leicestershire to south-east England, both for building new motorways and for the construction industry generally. Foster Yeoman's output grew to the extent that BR traction had to be used once again for traffic out of Merehead, pending the construction of a fifth Class 59 locomotive in the USA. Several roadstone terminals were either inaugurated or modernised during 1988, whilst the Channel Tunnel terminal at Sevington, opened in November 1987, started receiving regular trains from Whatley, Cliffe and Snowdown. A surprise innovation in May 1988 was the Redland self-discharge train, allowing deliveries to be made to terminals with no underfloor discharge facilities.The Petroleum sub-sector scored a success in March 1988 with a 'jumbo train' from Immingham to Nottingham, possibly paving the way for many more double length trains on trunk routes. Railfreight Coal is now carrying more of its staple commodity than before the miners' strike, and although the number of rail-served collieries and patent fuel plants continues to decrease, the overall position at the end of 1988 was a healthy one. Several more block train flows were converted to air braked operation during the year, and domestic coal to Scotland, Ireland and one London depot (West Drayton) continued to benefit from the use of containers. Perhaps the most significant events of 1988 for Railfreight Coal were those happening in Scotland, where new flows of imported coal brought rail traffic back to Rothesay Dock and (for a time) Kincardine, and a resurgence of domestic/export traffic brought two line reopenings: first the Annbank–Mauchline link in March, and then the Waterside branch in the autumn. There was a welcome boost for Railfreight Coal in North East England, too, with a new flow from Butterwell to ICI Wilton expected to amount to 500,000 tonnes a year. The Metals sub-sector managed to increase its market share of steel traffic in 1988, with more specialised wagons coming into use for the conveyance of cold reduced coil and certain other products. One of the best publicised landmarks for Railfreight Metals in 1988 was not connected with steel at all: this was the £2.4 m. investment scheme by British Alcan, providing new terminal facilities at its Lochaber works and new pressurised wagons for the alumina traffic from Blyth.

So much for the bulk traffics; what of Railfreight Distribution? Here the main feature of 1988 was the merger in October with Freightliner, designed to bring all non-bulk traffic flows under a single administration. Previously Freightliner had been a wholly owned subsidiary of the BRB, functioning independently of the main Railfreight business. Impetus for the merger came partly from the prospect of vastly increased traffic after opening of the Channel Tunnel in 1993; no longer would Railfreight and Freightliner be competing for the same traffic, but rather the combined organisation would offer the customer whichever system was best suited to his requirements. One practical consequence of the merger was expected to be the joint operation of certain train services; indeed the dust had hardly settled on the new organisation when a new link was inaugurated between Bristol and Coatbridge, with Freightliner wagons conveyed by scheduled Speedlink workings.

Looking at specific traffic flows, there were both losses and gains during 1988, but the Speedlink network remained little changed since the closure of the Severn Tunnel Junction yards in November 1987. Particular areas of growth were Norsk Hydro fertiliser from Immingham and raw timber from Scotland and South East England, the latter including some new destinations such as Llandudno Junction (temporarily) and Chirk. Even before opening of the Channel Tunnel BR is keen to increase its share of cross-channel freight traffic, and some important strides in this direction were made during the summer. Firstly, a new ship was commissioned on the Dover–Dunkerque route, with sufficient railway wagon capacity to attract new trainload flows as well as improving the transit time of Speedlink traffic. At the same time, the existing ferry terminal at Dover was replaced by a new, more conveniently situated one. For the future, Railfreight Distribution is increasingly looking to intermodal and container systems as a means of attracting new traffic; one of these systems, Minilink, was in regular operation for much of the year between London (Willesden) and Glasgow (Deanside).

The main development in the Parcels sector in 1988 was, sadly, a negative one. The network of newspaper trains from production centres in London and Manchester was abandoned in July, after successive withdrawals of custom by publishers had made the network unviable. Just one or two titles would continue to be carried by passenger or general parcels trains. The remainder of the sector's operations continued to operate successfully, however, with BR's own Red Star service still attracting a good level of business. The network of Travelling Post Office trains was revamped in May and October, resulting in the loss of mail trains to and from Aberdeen but providing new links to Dover and across central London. In common with Provincial and Network SouthEast, the Parcels sector is replacing many locomotive-hauled workings with multiple unit trains, enabling significant cost savings to be made. The majority of the parcels unit fleet had been concentrated on Cambridge depot by the end of the year, although their duties take them far and wide on the BR system.

▲During the second half of 1988 all the Class 47 locomotives used on Stanlow oil traffic were repainted in new-style Railfreight Petroleum livery and named in Latin after shells. No. 47085 *Conidae* crosses Gauxholme viaduct near Todmorden with the 12.14 Jarrow–Stanlow 'empties' on 16th August. This particular locomotive was formerly named *Mammoth* as one of the original batch of Western Region named Class 47s. *Les Nixon*

NEW SERVICES

◀ In connection with Channel Tunnel construction traffic from the Trans-Manche Link terminal at Grain, Class 33/0 locomotives Nos. 33050 and 33051 were named *Isle of Grain* and *Shakespeare Cliff* respectively on 16th May. Both had previously been repainted in Railfreight Construction livery. The pair is seen departing from the TML site with a train of concrete lining segments shortly after the naming ceremony. Visible in the background is the BP storage depot which generates a modest amount of bitumen and fuel oil traffic. *Brian Morrison*

▲The quarry terminal at Penmaenmawr has traditionally concentrated on the supply of railway ballast for North Wales and North West England, with only a small amount of revenue-earning traffic. A new addition to the freight schedule in February 1988 was a four times weekly revenue-earning train to Ashburys (Manchester), conveying granite chippings for use in the construction industry. Class 47 No. 47318 waits in the ARC sidings at Penmaenmawr on 7th April, almost ready to leave with 18.55 working to Ashburys. The wagons are 'grab discharge' POAs built on the underframes of redundant tank wagons and leased to ARC by Tiger Rail. *Paul Shannon*

▼The single track branch from Buxton to Hindlow received a welcome boost in early 1988 when a new flow of limestone from Tunstead to Hindlow commenced operation. Trains are scheduled to run twice daily in each direction, including Saturdays, Sundays and Bank Holidays. The route involves reversals at both Buxton and Peak Forest, the latter being necessary because there is no direct access from Tunstead Works towards Buxton. The ICI terminal at Hindlow is illustrated after a light spring snowfall on Saturday 9th April, with Class 37/5 locomotives Nos. 37679 and 37683 present on the 09.15 service from Tunstead. *Paul Shannon*

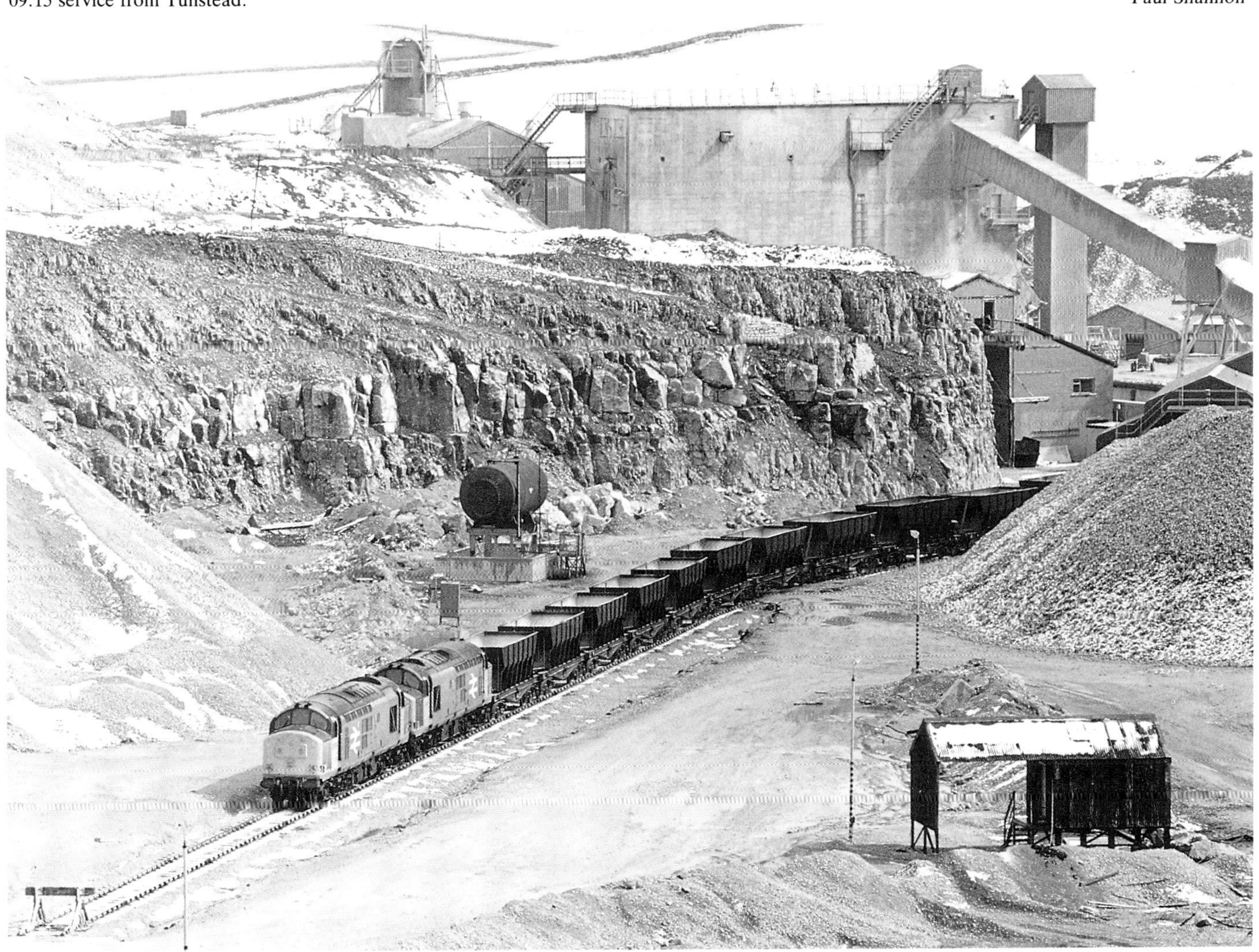

▲One of Railfreight Distribution's success stories in the late 1980s is the carriage of bulk fertiliser from the Norsk Hydro plant at Immingham. Block trains run from Immingham to Avonmouth and Leith, and there is also Speedlink traffic to several destinations including Alscott, Ashford (Kent), Holton Heath, Banbury and Aberdeen. The partnership between BR and this particular customer was acknowledged in March 1988 when Class 47 locomotive No. 47319 was named Norsk Hydro, No. 47319 living up to its name on 27th May when photographed passing Wrawby Junction with empty vans for Immingham, including some of the latest curtain–sided vehicles. Many of the vans used for Norsk Hydro traffic are registered abroad and leased to Isis Link by the German firm Cargowaggon, although their operations are normally confined to the British mainland. *Les Nixon*

▲Inverurie yard is one of the locations transformed by the burgeoning timber traffic to Shotton and Irvine. On 28th July 1988 Class 47 No. 47316 acts as yard pilot after arriving with a 'trip' freight (6A03) from Aberdeen Guild Street. On the left are a variety of OTA timber wagons waiting to be loaded with local produce, some of which lies in a small pile in the centre of the yard. Coupled to the locomotive are an empty china clay tank from Port Elphinstone to Quidhampton (near Salisbury) and eleven loaded OTAs from Inverurie to Irvine. *Michael Rhodes*

►Towards the end of 1987 two roadstone terminals were established in the down sidings at Woking, one to receive ARC traffic from Whatley and the other Redland traffic from Merehead. By May 1988 trains from both quarries had earned themselves a place in the regular freight schedule, with three booked trains a week from each quarry. A visit to Woking on 4th July found No. 56052 (left) shunting loaded PTA wagons from Whatley whilst sister locomotive No. 56070 (right) stood at the head of empty POAs for Merehead. The use of the flat-bottomed wagons on both services, emptied by mechanical grab, meant that existing sidings could be used at Woking without the need for substantial investment in hopper discharge equipment. *Paul Shannon*

◄The driver and guard of No. 47079 discuss operations at the Plasmor terminal at Great Heck before continuing their journey to Doncaster Belmont on 27th June 1988. The train is the 10.40 Speedlink 'trip' from Selby. On the right are Peter Scott of the Railway Civil Engineers and Geoff Nicols of the PRO at York, discussing future plans for this thriving location. By 1988 Plasmor traffic had grown sufficiently to warrant the conversion of 30 open wagons specifically for this firm's traffic; one of the prototype vehicles is visible immediately behind the locomotive. *B.J.Nicolle*

►With construction work well advanced on the A55 North Wales trunk road, Railfreight was able to carry substantial amounts of steel, cement and sand to the site during 1988. Most of the A55 traffic is offloaded at a purpose-built terminal at Conwy Morfa, but some use is also made of Llandudno Junction freight depot. This busy scene at Llandudno Junction was captured on 18th May 1988, with No. 08472 shunting a rake of BDA steel carriers from Cardiff; these were later 'tripped' along the main line to Conwy Morfa. Also visible in the background are No. 47531 with the Amlwch–Ellesmere Port chemicals train and No. 47307 with the daily Speedlink trip from Holyhead. *Don Gatehouse*

▲Tha January 1988 freight timetable supplement saw the incorporation of a new Speedlink Coal service from Coedbach Washery to Mossend, routed in both directions via Hereford, Shrewsbury and the West Coast main line. The service runs on Saturdays only, using resources which would otherwise be standing idle. The sole traffic is anthracite duff for an industrial plant near Motherwell, which is carried in HDA merry-go-round wagons. The loaded train, the 08.40 departure from Coedbach, is seen passing Cardiff on 17th December behind the aptly named No. 37235 *Coal Merchants' Association of Scotland*. *Don Gatehouse*

◀Revenue-earning freight returned to the Westbury–Yeovil–Exeter route in January 1988 when the three times weekly Speedlink Coal service from Washwood Heath to Exmouth Junction was re-routed that way. The purpose of the re-routeing was to serve a new coal concentration depot at Yeovil Junction. The return 'empties' kept their former route from Exmouth Junction to Radyr via Taunton and Bristol. The loaded train is pictured at Yeovil Pen Mill on 14th October behind Class 37/3 No. 37376, one of Cardiff Canton's dedicated fleet for Speedlink Coal traffic. From January 1989 this working was due to be further amended, starting from Radyr instead of Washwood Heath and calling at Stonehouse en route as well as Yeovil. *Rodney Lissenden*

▶New motorways can be good news for Railfreight during the construction phase, even if in the longer term they pose a threat to the railway as a whole. The year 1988 saw frequent stone trains running from both Merehead and Mountsorrel to the M40 railhead at Banbury. The 11.30 departure from Merehead to Banbury is pictured near Frome on Saturday 6th August, with Class 56 No. 56051 providing the traction. The wagons used on this service are two-axle POAs leased from Tiger Rail. *Don Gatehouse*

SCOTRAIL REVIVALS

▲The mothballed line between Mauchline and Annbank was reopened on 17th March for use by Knockshinnoch–Ayr Harbour coal trains. The cost of the reopening was met by the Coal sub-sector alone, and for the time being at least all other trains between Carlisle and Ayrshire continued to travel via Kilmarnock. Class 20s Nos. 20193 and 20192 are pictured breaking the ceremonial banner at Mauchline on the day of the line's reopening. ScotRail General Manager John Ellis is the tall gentleman on the platform on the right. *Tom Noble*

▼Trains to and from the reopened Rothesay Dock terminal on the north bank of the River Clyde have to thread their way through Yoker carriage depot in order to gain access to the branch.On 11th July Class 26s Nos. 26007 and 26004 negotiate Yoker sidings as they approach their destination with the 10.05 'empties' from Kincardine. Trains to Kincardine were composed of manual discharge HEA hopper wagons instead of the merry-go-round HAA variety because the automatic discharge equipment at Kincardine was not operative. *Paul Shannon*

ROLLING STOCK OLD....

▲The dwindling ranks of vacuum-braked HTV hopper wagons became even scarcer in 1988, with several flows going over to air-braked operation during the year. Class 47 No. 47050 approaches Edale with a rake of empty HTVs on 17th August, forming the 08.00 'special' from Ely to Peak Forest (6Z61). By that time the use of HTVs on Peak District limestone trains was limited to 'specials' to Ely and Selby, with equally antiquated MSVs surviving on the daily train to Leeds. *Paul Shannon*

◀By the beginning of 1988 most long distance coal trains had gone over to air braked operation, using 'merry-go-round' type HAA hoppers. One vacuum-braked service which lingered on until the summer, however, was the flow from Holditch (Staffordshire) to British Steel Llanwern. A busy scene at Silverdale, on the Holditch branch, is depicted on the morning of 13th April, as Class 20s Nos. 20113 and 20055 pause with a rake of empty MDVs for Holditch. On the right, a merry-go-round train from Silverdale to Ironbridge is awaiting authority to proceed down the branch to Madeley. *Paul Shannon*

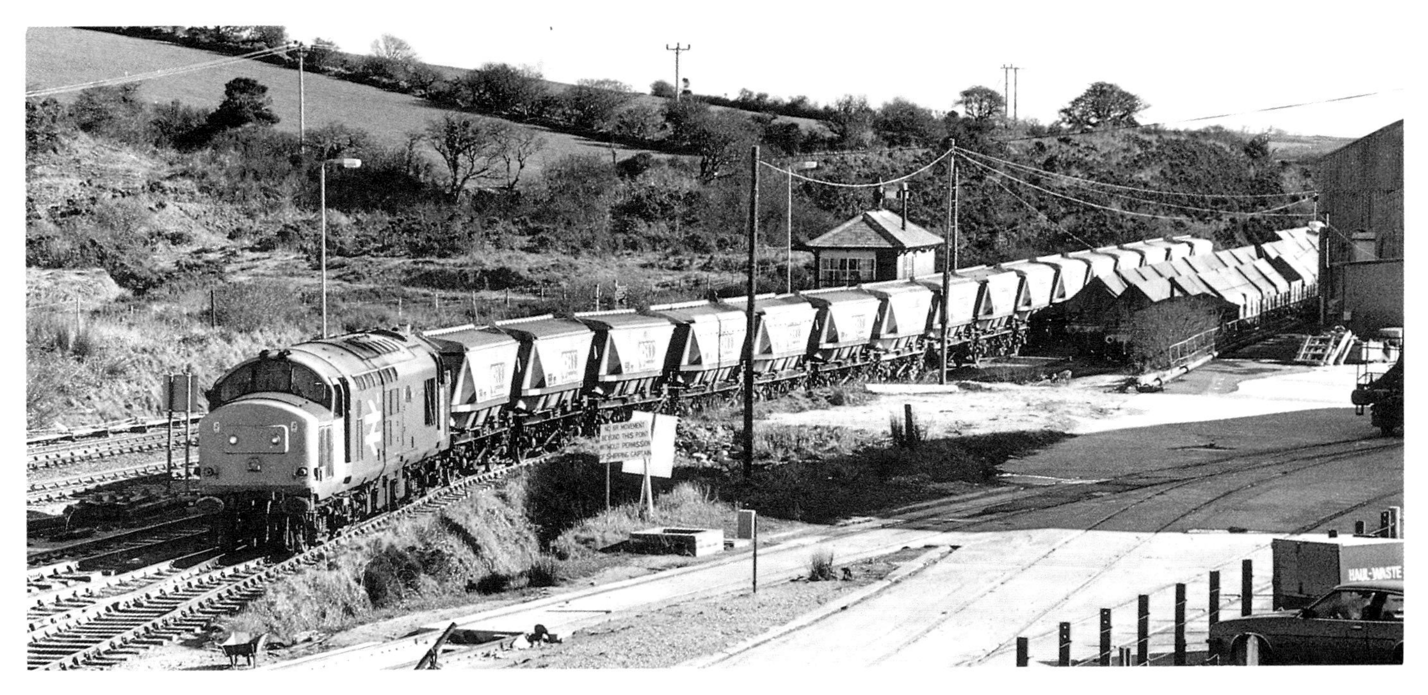

...AND NEW

▲The changing scene in Cornwall ... Class 37/5 No. 37675 has just arrived at Rocks Driers (Goonbarrow) on the morning of 16th February, hauling a rake of empty CDAs from Fowey. Rocks is the busiest loading point for Fowey traffic, accounting for 60% of the total tonnage railed to the port. The use of modern loading apparatus ensures that wagon turnround times are kept to a minimum; in this case No. 37675 will wait whilst its train is loaded and then head straight back to St Blazey for a shift change. On the right are some of the previous generation of 'clay hoods', awaiting their final journey to the scrapyard. *Paul Shannon*

◄The ECC clay discharge terminal at Fowey is illustrated on 15th February 1988, with one CDA wagon about to be discharged (right) and several more returning empty to the exchange sidings (left). Lineside apparatus is used to automatically unlock and open the wagon doors prior to discharge, and the traverser visible in the foreground is used to transfer wagons between adjacent tracks. *Paul Shannon*

►Scrap metal traffic from Ardwick to Cardiff (Allied Steel & Wire) benefited from the introduction of air-braked POAs in early 1988, replacing the last of the BR-owned MDVs on this traffic. The POAs also carry scrap to Cardiff from Trafford Park, Snailwell and Exeter, travelling by a mixture of block trains and scheduled Speedlink services. Two empty POAs for Ardwick comprise the 14.16 Warrington–Ashburys Speedlink 'trip' on 15th April, seen approaching Ordsall Lane Junction behind Class 47 No. 47207 *Bulmers of Hereford*. *Paul Shannon*

◄Amongst the oldest wagons in revenue-earning service on BR are the ICI hoppers used on limestone trains out of Tunstead. Some of these vehicles are over half a century old and still giving excellent service. Their main use is on the three times daily Industrial Minerals subsector trains to Lostock and Oakleigh, but they also carry roadstone to three Manchester terminals and internal traffic to ICI Hindlow. Haulage for the Tunstead–Oakleigh trains is normally provided from the 'trainload' pool of Class 47s at Crewe, whilst the other trains are mostly covered by pairs of Class 37/5s based at Tinsley. Class 47 No. 47318 approaches Peak Forest on 12th August with the 11.47 Oakleigh–Tunstead 'empties'. *Paul Shannon*

MERRY-GO-ROUND CONVERSIONS

▲During 1988 the coal services to Abercwmboi Phurnacite plant went over to MGR operation. This involved the introduction of HAA hoppers on trains from Tower and Methyr Vale collieries. Here a rake of 20 HAAs arrives at Merthyr Vale on 19th October behind Class 37/7 No. 37796. The train will be loaded in two sections from a small 'pad' constructed earlier in the year when rail access to the pit was simplified to allow direct BR access from the junction at Black Lion. *Michael Rhodes*

▼Westoe pit in South Shields was another colliery to benefit from the introduction of a new MGR service during 1988. In the summer holidays during August the trackwork from Dean exchange sidings was resignalled to allow British Rail direct access into the mine for the first time in its eighty year history. On 31st August Class 56 No. 56121 is pictured running round its train, the J16 'trip' from Sunderland South Dock. It will propel the 36 HAA hoppers into the siding next to the loading pad where they will be filled in about 45 minutes. The new BR service from Westoe has led to the end of coal exports through the nearby Harton staithes, although the staithes are still used for dumping shale at sea. *Michael Rhodes*

▲Air braked hoppers also took over the Fen Drayton–Kings Cross sand traffic early in 1988. In this case the train is still scheduled to run daily, but using high-capacity Tiger PHAs (formerly coded PBA) instead of BR-owned HTVs. Some of the traffic is still detached at Alexandra Palace en route. This picture shows Class 31s Nos. 31250 and 31135 taking the Hertford loop line at Langley Junction with the loaded train on 25th March. *Paul Shannon*

▼At last converted to air-braked wagon stock during 1988 was the Marks Tey–Mile End sand traffic. This had been one of the last vacuum-braked freight services on the Anglia Region. On 19th October the new stock passes Marks Tey station behind Class 31s Nos. 31308 and 31294, having worked to Mile End and back during the morning. One of the 'bonuses' of the new stock is that the train runs less frequently than before – usually three times a week. Note the graffiti on the leading wagon – surely the problem of 1988! *Michael J. Collins*

YARDS FOR SPEEDLINK

▲Marshalling yard retrenchment – The extensive hump yard at Temple Mills has been reduced to a small group of sidings on the site of the former 'C' and 'D' fans, on the east side of the realigned Stratford–Tottenham Hale line. Most Speedlink traffic for East London is sent via Willesden or Ripple Lane yards, but Temple Mills remains in use as a collecting point for several local terminals, including Bow, Silvertown, Gidea Park and Stratford (LIFT). On 7th July 1988 Class 47 No. 47157 prepares to leave Temple Mills with the 17.35 departure to Willesden; this will in turn feed into a Willesden–Dover service. The tank wagons on the adjacent track will form the 18.35 'trip' to Ripple Lane, connecting with an overnight Ripple Lane–Tees Yard service. On the right is a rake of empty HEA coal hoppers from Bow, waiting to return to Didcot on the next Speedlink Coal working. *Paul Shannon*

▼And marshalling yard renaissance – Cardiff Tidal sidings have actually seen an increase in traffic during 1988, having taken over some of the work previously handled at Severn Tunnel Junction. Most of the traffic seen in this photograph of 15th July belongs to the Metals sub-sector, which is indeed responsible for two thirds of the yard's costs. Wagon types illustrated include HEA, TTA, BDA, OBA, BBA, HAA, VGA, SPA and MDV.

Michael Rhodes

SERVICES WITHDRAWN

▲The last day of rail operation to British Industrial Sand at Oakamoor on 30th August produced a pair of Class 20s, Nos. 20020 and 20132, for the scheduled train of PAA hoppers to St Helens. The incoming 'empties', running as the 12.16 from Stoke, are pictured near Endon on their last journey to the doomed terminus. Latterly the daily booked working had been running only once or twice a week, as British Industrial Sand gradually transferred their remaining Staffordshire output to road transport. The branch from Stoke to Leek Brook Junction remains open for aggregates traffic from Caldon Low, though the vacuum-braked wagons still used on this service are rapidly approaching the end of their working life.
Brian Morrison

►Relief driver Lionel Shaw and shunter Rex Taft pose for the photographer at BIS Oakamoor on 30th August, whilst the last railborne consignment of sand is loaded into the company's PAA hoppers. All shunting operations at Oakamoor were carried out by *Brightside*, the 0-4-0 shunter illustrated here. *T.R. Moors*

◄Class 31 No. 31271 stands at the end of the Blodwell branch on 14th September, ready to depart with the 15.45 ballast train to Bescot. The contract for this traffic expired in the autumn, and the 7½-mile branch from Gobowen was effectively closed after the last ballast train ran on 28th October. The recovery of track and signalling was, however, to be delayed until the possibility of further freight contracts for the line had been explored. *Brian Morrison*

◄The last scheduled train on the Radstock branch passes near the site of Mells Road station on 29th June, headed by Class 47 No. 47370. Latterly the branch had remained open only to serve the Marcroft wagon repair works at Radstock, and the daily 'trip' working from Westbury would normally comprise no more than two or three wagons. The train pictured here included some BR wagons carrying materials from the site as well as the residue of privately-owned wagons repaired by Marcroft.
Michael Mensing

▼Between autumn 1987 and summer 1988 the Greater Manchester 'bin liners' ran to Wakefield instead of Appley Bridge, pending an expansion of the landfill site at the latter location. During this period the transfer station at Northenden continued to despatch rail traffic as normal, but the use of Dean Lane and Brindle Heath was suspended and Bredbury served instead. Trains ran each weekday from both Northenden and Bredbury to Wakefield and back, routed via Hebden Bridge. Class 47/3 No.47344 approaches Stockport on 14th April with the 12.08 Wakefield–Northenden 'empties'. On the left is another sight to disappear from Stockport during 1988 – an HST set on the 08.40 Plymouth–Manchester Piccadilly service.
Paul Shannon

◄The daily Didcot–Chessington coal train was discontinued in December 1988, bringing to an end the sight of Class 37s on the Chessington branch. The traffic was expected to be hauled by road from Purley in future. Class 37/0 No. 37131 passes West Ealing on 31st October with the 14.52 Chessington–Didcot 'empties', comprising a larger number of wagons than was usual for this service.
Paul Shannon

LOCOMOTIVE TOPICS

▲Although electrification was extended to several freight terminals in East London during 1988, most freight trains over the North London line continued to be diesel hauled. Regular electric haulage was limited to the two car-carrying trains in each direction between Dagenham and Halewood, normally attracting Class 85 traction but with occasional appearances of Classes 81 and 86/5. Class 85 No. 85016 passes Highbury & Islington with the 12.45 Fords train from Dagenham on 7th July. *Paul Shannon*

▼The end of double-headed Class 56s on South Wales iron ore trains was heralded in summer 1988 when pairs of refurbished Class 37s began appearing on these workings. On 21st July Class 37/5 No.37697 and Class 37/7 No. 37889, painted in 'old' and 'new' style Railfreight liveries respectively, are pictured leaving the British Steel complex at Llanwern with the 15.00 'empties' to Port Talbot. At this stage the substitution of Class 37s for Class 56s was still experimental. *Michael Rhodes*

▲Class 20s Nos. 20040 and 20170 roll into Aberystwyth station on 6th April with the Wednesdays-only 01.16 oil train from Stanlow. The use of Class 20s on this service finished not long after this photograph was taken, with the last recorded working occurring on 11th May.

Paul Shannon

◄After departure of the Class 20s, the weekly Aberystwyth oil train was rostered for Class 37/4 haulage west of Shrewsbury, bringing it in line with all other loco-hauled trains on Cambrian lines. This photograph shows No. 37430 approaching Dovey Junction with the 15.24 'empties' from Aberystwyth on 7th September. It had been thought that the train would be retimed to operate between Shrewsbury and Aberystwyth during the night, taking advantage of the radio signalling installed on the line, but this had not taken place by the end of the year.

Don Gatehouse

▼Foster Yeoman Class 59 No. 59003 *Yeoman Highlander* passes South Croydon on 7th June with the 09.53 Crawley–Merehead stone 'empties'. During the year the scope of Class 59 operation was extended to both Crawley and Harlow, so that all Foster Yeoman's London area terminals may now be reached by this class. *David Brown*

►**Two of the five remaining Class 03 diesel-mechanical shunters ended up on the Isle of Wight. On 9th December the two of them Nos. 03079 in Rail blue livery and 03179 in Network SouthEast livery were seen stabled outside Ryde depot.** *Brian Denton*

▼**Agreement was made during 1988 to sell the BR-owned Vale of Rheidol Light Railway to the Brecon Mountain Railway, although the sale had not been concluded by the end of the year. Meanwhile, the line's first diesel locomotive entered service. Here No. 10 is seen on an Aberystwyth–Devil's Bridge test run at Capel Bangor.** *Andrew Bannister*

▲**On summer saturdays during 1988, a pair of Buxton-based Class 37/5s were rostered to work passenger trains on the Cambrian route. Nos. 37682 and 37683 make a fine sight at Commins Coch on 21st May, the first Saturday of operation, with the 10.10 Aberystwyth–Euston.** *Andrew Bannister*

DEMISE OF THE 'PEAKS'

▲The Class 45 'Peaks' were all withdrawn during 1988 after 28 years of service. 45012, one of the formerly steam-heated Class 45/0 sub-class is seen on a wintry 22nd January at Healey Mills Yard with a short train of hoppers. *David Rodgers*

◀The electric train-heat-fitted Class 45/1 were regular performers on the Newcastle–Poole service until all remaining members of the class were withdrawn on 27th July. Five days later No. 45106 was reinstated by the InterCity sector and eventually repainted in green livery. It is seen on 5th November on the Pathfinder Tours 'Wessex Adventurer' railtour at Marchwood. *Brian Denton*

THE PARCELS SCENE

▲Friday 8th July 1988 was the last day of the West of England newspaper train, and a special arrangement was made for the 'empties' to be double-headed by Class 50s Nos. 50001 *Dreadnought* and 50015 *Valiant* from Plymouth. The pair is pictured near Dawlish. *Reg Jones*

▼With the loss of newspaper traffic in July 1988 came the demise of a number of long-standing van trains emanating from both London and Manchester. The return 'empties' mostly ran during daylight hours and tended to be better known than the loaded workings. The last ever working of the Cleethorpes–Longsight 'empties' waits at Sheffield Midland on 4th July, with traction provided by Class 31/4 No. 31428 *The North Yorkshire Moors Railway*. *Peter Fox*

▲A Class 127 parcels unit stands at Bristol Bath Road depot on 31st October, prior to departing with a driver training run to Taunton. These units were due to enter service on several long-distance parcels workings at the end of November, replacing locomotive-hauled formations on routes to Manchester, Cardiff and Southampton. *Mike Goodfield*

◄The first Class 419 Motor Luggage Van to receive Royal Mail red livery was No. 9004. It is seen freshly outshopped from Selhurst on 28th October 1988. *Brian Morrison*

▼Royal Mail livery was also applied to several Class 128 diesel parcel cars during 1988. No. 55992 passes through the carriage washer at Old Oak Common on 18th June. *Michael J. Collins*

LOCOMOTIVES

1988 saw many changes in the locomotive fleet, with probably the most significant development occurring on 17th May when the official contract for the construction of 100 Class 60 freight locomotives was placed with Brush Electrical Machines (BEM) of Loughborough. At the end of the year the body of No. 60001 was taking shape at subcontractors Procor Ltd and on schedule for a June 1989 delivery.

The previous year's sub-sectorisation of the traction fleet was further developed with many operation-led fleets formed, such as a batch of Class 31s allocated to Crewe's FHHA pool for nuclear flask coal traffic.

On 12th February the first Class 91 No. 91001 was handed over by GEC Transportation Ltd to the BRB in a special roll-out ceremony held at BREL Crewe.

Key features were: 140 mph capability; high availability; low unsprung mass by virtue of having body-mounted traction motors suspended in the space between the bogie frames; microprocessor control of power supply, wheel slip, motor power equality and interfacing with the time division multiplex equipment (remote control of the loco from the DVT using train wires). As with expensive cars, this locomotive has ' on-board diagnostics' - the microprocessor stores fault information for easier maintenance.

▼The first Class 91 electric locomotive for ECML operation, No. 91001 was finished by GEC/BREL during January, and handed over to BR in a special 'roll-out' held at Crewe Works on 12th February. The locomotive, with its No. 1 end leading poses in the works yard. Note the GEC legend applied to the buffers. *Peter Fox*

►John Prideaux, Director InterCity, is obviously pleased with his new loco, as he stands in the cab doorway. *Peter Fox*

The Class 91 appeared in February's Channel 4 programme: 'Equinox: Running To Time'. This programme, produced by Paul Fabricus, highlighted the intensifying battle between BR, domestic airlines and coaches for inter-city business travel. The Class 91 was to take over from the HST as BR's main weapon. Hopefully, it will do for InterCity in the 1990s what the HST has succeeded in doing in the late 1970s and 1980s.

On 14th February the locomotive commenced testing firstly in the Crewe area, and after a few days was transferred to the Engineering Development Unit at the Railway Technical Centre, Derby, for type testing. After several days at Derby No. 91001 hauled by a Class 47, was taken to the Old Dalby Test Track and in conjunction with RDB975422 'Prometheus' commenced pantograph and ride tests. By the end of March the second of the build was delivered direct to Bounds Green depot and was soon joined by No. 91001. Once on the Eastern Region equipment and performance testing was carried out jointly by GEC Traction, the DM&EE and BR Research. By the end of 1988 all 10 of the pilot order had been delivered to Bounds Green, but did not enter passenger service at the year end, because of software 'bugs' discovered whilst testing on the East Coast Main Line. To permit operation of Class 91 locomotives, prior to the introduction of the Metro-Cammell Mark 4 Driving Van Trailers, a further 8 conventional Class 43 locomotives were fitted with tdm equipment to enable remote multiple with Class 91 locomotives

Brush prototype 25kV Co-Co electric locomotive No. 89001 became a resident at Bounds Green Depot from early in the year, with its distinctive body lines becoming a regular sight on the ECML. After the necessary training and line testing 89001 took part in the Hamburg Exhibition during May, and after returning to the UK was again allocated to BN. 89001's entry into passenger service came on 3rd July when it was selected to haul the *MALLARD* 50th anniversary special from King's Cross to Doncaster and return. From 15th July the locomotive commenced operating the 07.16 Peterborough–Kings Cross and 17.36 return service hauling a complete HST formation with a tdm equipped Class 43, in order to provide three-phase supply to the coaches – although the 89 is not itself tdm fitted. During the late summer and autumn the Class 89 and its high speed formation operated various test and passenger diagrams, including infrequent appearances on duties between King's Cross & Leeds.

Due to teething problems with the GEC Class 90 locomotives their introduction into revenue earning service was considerably delayed with the first recorded passenger duty occurring on 12th July when No. 90003 piloted Class 86/4 No. 86413 on the 13.40 Blackpool North–Euston forward from Crewe.

▲One of the bogies of 91001, showing one of the angled body-slung traction motors immediately to the right of the large secondary coil springs.
Peter Fox

▲After the introduction of the Class 89 into regular service on the ECML, the locomotive became regularly deployed on the 07.16 Peterborough–King's Cross and 17.36 return service. The train's formation was an HST set, marshalled with a Time Division Multiplex-fitted HST power car at the London end. Due to the Class 89 not being fitted with TDM the locomotive always had to lead the formation when in passenger service. The 07.16 Peterborough service is seen at the blocks at King's Cross on 15th September.
Brian Morrison

► In early 1988 a number of driver training runs were operated on the ECML, using the Class 89 with a rake of spare Mark 1 and Mark 2 vehicles, on 18th January being seen passing St. Neots. During the summer No. 89001 was repainted in original InterCity colours prior to its exhibition in Hamburg. *Ian Cowley*

◄▲By late April Bound's Green depot had taken delivery of its first Class 91, from where, after driver training had taken place, the locomotives embarked upon a major proving programme. Reasons were two-fold, to train drivers on their new charges, and to prove new equipment including the locomotive's computer software. On 2nd June, No. 91002 passes Huntingdon on a return test special with its No. 2 end leading. *Ian Cowley*

◄The outward journey of the above test run, also at Huntingdon. *Ian Cowley*

►A unique event occurred on 27th June when the first Class 90, No. 90005 *Financial Times* visited King's Cross. The purpose of the locomotive's operation on ER was in connection with line testing of the recently-electrified ECML section. The locomotive is seen standing at the buffer stops at 05.39, prior to running light to Bounds Green. *Ken Brunt*

At the commencement of 1988 only 25 of the once 127 strong fleet of Class 45 'Peak' locomotives remained and all were withdrawn by 2nd August. No. 45106 was reinstated two days later by Tinsley depot, and repainted into Brunswick green livery, with the depot's cast White Rose logo being applied under the assistant driver's windows. No. 45106 is now allocated to the InterCity Charter sub-sector for charter and special duties. However, the locomotive saw regular use from October on the 07.12 Derby–St. Pancras and 17.50 return service.

As well as being available for ordinary InterCity duties, No. 45106 was the star attraction at a number of autumn open days.

▲For the last months of their lives the Class 45s were allocated to Tinsley depot, Sheffield, and could be found operating freight traffic in the Midlands and Yorkshire area, as well as occasional passenger services. On 9th July, No. 45128 departs from Doncaster past Hexthorpe with the 07.22 Newcastle–Weymouth, the 'Peak' operating as far as Birmingham. *Colin J. Marsden*

▼With enthusiasts peering from virtually every door window, No. 45141 passes along the sea wall between Dawlish and Dawlish Warren on 4th June with the 12.10 Paignton–Rose Grove service. *Reg Jones*

On 7th July the 07.05 Derby–Paignton excursion was hauled by 45141, and is seen passing Bromsgrove. *Steve Turner*

►In the autumn, MC Metals of Glasgow purchased a number of Class 45s for scrap. After purchase locomotives were moved to BRML Glasgow for disposal. As a number of locomotives still contained blue asbestos the adjacent former BRML asbestos plant, now owned by MCM, was used to remove this deadly substance. In November Nos. 45001/2/4/10/26/48/49/51/ 70 had arrived for dismantling. No. 45048 and the remains of No. 45001 are seen in the illustration. *Paul Gash*

By the end of the year many 'Peaks' plus the odd Class 47 had begun to congregate at Tinsley Yard awaiting disposal. The photograph shows 45012/33/37/46/52/77/103/107/110/113/115/120/124/134/140/141/145/ 150. 46009. 47073/104. 97405/10–13 and ADB 968024. *Les Nixon*

The pioneer Class 37 No. D6700, latterly 37119, received a CEM intermediate overhaul at BREL Crewe between January and March. In addition to the installation of re-geared CP7 bogies, and being renumbered 37350, the locomotive was repainted into BR green livery with full yellow ends. In addition to its TOPS number, the original number D6700 was applied. At the year end 37350 was allocated to the Railfreight Petroleum Cardiff pool (FPLW).

The original English Electric type 4 No. D200 (40122) finally went to rest in 1988 when after operating a number of railtours during the spring it powered an InterCity charter tour from Liverpool Street to York on 16th April, and took up its rightful place in the National Railway Museum. The locomotive was retained in a fully operational condition but did not leave the museum in 1988. Prior to the operation of its final tours No. D200 was repainted by Stratford major depot, and the tour on 12th March entitled 'Pennine Forty Farewell' was operated with the locomotive in grey primer!

Although D200 was the last Class 40 in capital stock it was not the last to operate under its own power on BR metals, as on 6th September No. 40135 travelled from Tyseley to Leicester under its own power en route to Vic Berry's for asbestos removal. The locomotive was eventually purchased by the Class 40 Preservation Society at Bury.

The general run-down of the Class 50 fleet continued in 1988 with the final 'F' exam being given to No. 50003 *Temeraire* at Laira during March. From that date the largest routine examination programmed for the Class 50s was an 'E', scheduled for every 5,000 service hours. To provide a pool of spares and eliminate locomotives that were due for overhaul , a total of five Class 50s Nos. 50010/13/22/38/47 were withdrawn during the year. It is sad to record that the first member of the fleet was cut up during the year when No. 50006 *Neptune* withdrawn in July 1987 was broken up at Vic Berry's scrapyard in Leicester during March.

After much speculation about the formation of a 86/5 sub-class, the first example appeared from BREL Crewe in May. Alterations mainly consisted of re-gearing for 75 mph operation. Allocation of the locomotives was to the Speedlink Freightliner pool.

◀ By the end of 1988 two withdrawn Class 50s were stored at Old Oak Common loco depot, Nos. 50013/38, both of which had supplied many components to other locomotives, indeed the power unit from No. 50038 was being reconditioned at Old Oak Common to provide the depot with a spare engine. This view shows No. 50038 dumped, devoid of its nameplates outside Old Oak Common loco depot in early December.
Colin J. Marsden

▼ One of the most popular classes with enthusiasts during 1988 was the Class 50, which were reduced by a further 5 examples during the year. In most cases their withdrawal was to supply spare parts to the two owning depots, who for the most of 1988 had machines out of service awaiting components. No. 50022 Anson was withdrawn with effect from 14.00 hours on 20th September following engine problems. On 20th August, the locomotive is seen hauling the 17.45 Exeter–Tavistock Junction engineers' train. *Colin J Marsden*

▲For the first time departmental-numbered locomotives have been used for passenger service, following the transfer of 4 Class 47/4s to the Research fleet. The locomotives were renumbered in 1988 in the 97XXX series and retained the last three digits of their original numbers. They are used for normal service when there is no work for them at the RTC. No. 97480 *Robin Hood* is seen at Nuneaton on 13th September, piloting Class 85 No. 85015 on a diverted Wolverhampton–Euston service. *A.O. Wynn*

►To enable more locomotives to traverse the increasing Radio Electronic Token Block network, several locomotives were RETB fitted during 1988. For the introduction of RETB equipment based at Banavie, near Fort William, three Class 20s were fitted with receiving/ transmitting equipment to enable freight operation in the Fort William area. One of the locomotives No. 20138 shows its RETB aerial on the nose end in this view at Fort William on 18th May. *Maxwell H. Fowler*

▼The reign of Class 03s on the mainland was reduced to just three operational examples during 1988 – all at Birkenhead, with the withdrawal of the Gateshead-based members. Newcastle station pilot duties were taken over by more conventional Class 08s. Although withdrawn, Nos. 03066/371/063/094 pose inside the shed at Gateshead on 30th May, looking in comparatively good condition. *Stephen Miller*

1988 saw the sale of Class 08s to both BREL (1988) Ltd and RFS Industries of Doncaster. BREL's purchase included Nos. 08168 for use at York and 08470 at Crewe. Those sold to RFS were No. 08331 for use at Doncaster which was repainted in a light blue colour scheme with yellow diamonds, while No. 08272/337 were sold to the same company to provide spare parts. BREL (1988) Ltd also became the owners of two Class 03s during the year when Nos. 03066/094 were sold for use at the company's Horwich foundry. The Horwich foundry was sold to the private sector in the autumn.

The first CEM overhaul for a Class 58 became due in 1988, this going to No. 58002, which received its attention at BRML Doncaster during January/February. When returned to traffic the locomotive was painted in Railfreight coal sub-sector colours. Still looking at the work of BRML Doncaster, the year saw the last HGO performed to a Class 31/1, No. 31106, which was returned to traffic on 26th March, painted in conventional blue livery.

◀The first Class 58 to receive a CEM overhaul was No. 58002 arriving in January. The overhaul of this locomotive was taken as an example to assess the time required for future classified repairs of this class. With power car removed, the body is seen in No. 4 bay on 20th January.
B.J. Nicolle

▶Railfreight locomotives, especially those allocated to Crewe TMD became 'labelled' with sticky plastic signs under the locomotive number indicating the operating fleet, during the early part of the year. No. 47187 sporting a label indicating membership of the Chemical Construction fleet, is shown at Derby station on a parcels train!
Colin J. Marsden

◀▼Looking striking in its new Railfreight subsector livery, Class 20 No. 20088 devoid of subsector identification stands in the works yard at BRML Doncaster on 8th July. This locomotive was repaired using many components from withdrawn collision-damaged sister locomotive No. 20077, with the Coal sector sponsoring the repair.
Colin J. Marsden

▶Although the introduction of the new Railfreight double grey livery was at the end of 1987, BREL Crewe works were still repainting Class 56s in the old colours until May 1988. The first of the Crewe repainted Class 56s No. 56069 is seen piloting Class 47/4 No. 47544 on the Irish Mail near Abergele on 24th May. *Larry Goddard*

▼BREL Crewe works has maintained its workload of Class 37 overhauls during the year, with full refurbishments and intermediate overhauls being performed. One which attracted much attention was to No. 37119 the pioneer of the class, which received an intermediate overhaul in February/March, this included the fitting of regeared CP7 bogies, and repainting into Brunswick green livery. The locomotive outshopped as No. 37350 is seen in the main works in mid-February in green undercoat.
Colin J. Marsden

▲After receiving serious accident damage, Class 31/4 No. 31401 was withdrawn. As the full complement of ETH fitted Class 31s was still required, the train supply equipment was removed and installed into locomotive No. 31161. Renumbering into the ETH batch was achieved by placing the locomotive at the head of the class as No. 31400. The choice of the 31400 number rather than 31470 was made as for maintenance purposes it was desirable to keep like equipped locomotives in numerical batches. The locomotive was outshopped in standard blue livery, although the body shell used of No. 31161 was previously in Railfreight colours. No. 31400 is seen on one of the turntable storage roads at Old Oak Common loco depot on 2nd July. *Michael J Collins*

Under the sector allocation of traction 4 Class 47/4s, Nos. 47472/480/ 545/561, were allocated to BR Research. In June these were allocated Departmental numbers 97414-417, but after consultation with the DM&EE the last three digits of the original numbers were retained, with just the first digit '4' being replaced by a '9', i.e. 47472 became 97472. The shortage of suitable main line motive power has meant that the Research Class 47s are regularly loaned to the InterCity and Provincial Sectors. One passenger duty often performed was the Friday's Only 15.40 Derby–St. Pancras and 18.20 return.

Because of extensive fire damage received by Class 47/7 No. 47713 *Tayside Region* in June, the decision was taken that repairs were uneconomical and withdrawal was authorised on 10th July. 47713 was taken to BRML Doncaster where all reusable components were removed. As ScotRail required the full complement of 16 push-pull Class 47s, a replacement No. 47497 was selected and converted to 47/7 No. 47717 at BRML Doncaster, being released in September. The nameplates *Tayside Region* were transferred to the new No. 47717. At the end of 1988 No.47713's body still languished at Doncaster.

The sole member of Class 47/9 No. 47901 normally deployed on Mendip stone duties, was called to BRML Doncaster for a general overhaul at the end of 1987, being returned to traffic in February 1988. Upon release the locomotive repainted in the new double-grey Railfreight colours and bearing the Construction sub-sector embellishments, returned to its old stamping ground. Unfortunately the availability of No. 47901 became very poor during the summer months with the locomotive being returned to BRML Doncaster for major rectification. At the close of the year the locomotive remained out of use at Doncaster.

The summer of 1988 saw the SEParately EXcited (SEPEX) traction motor project on Class 58 No. 58050 drawn to a close, with all non-standard equipment being removed on a visit to BRML Doncaster during July.

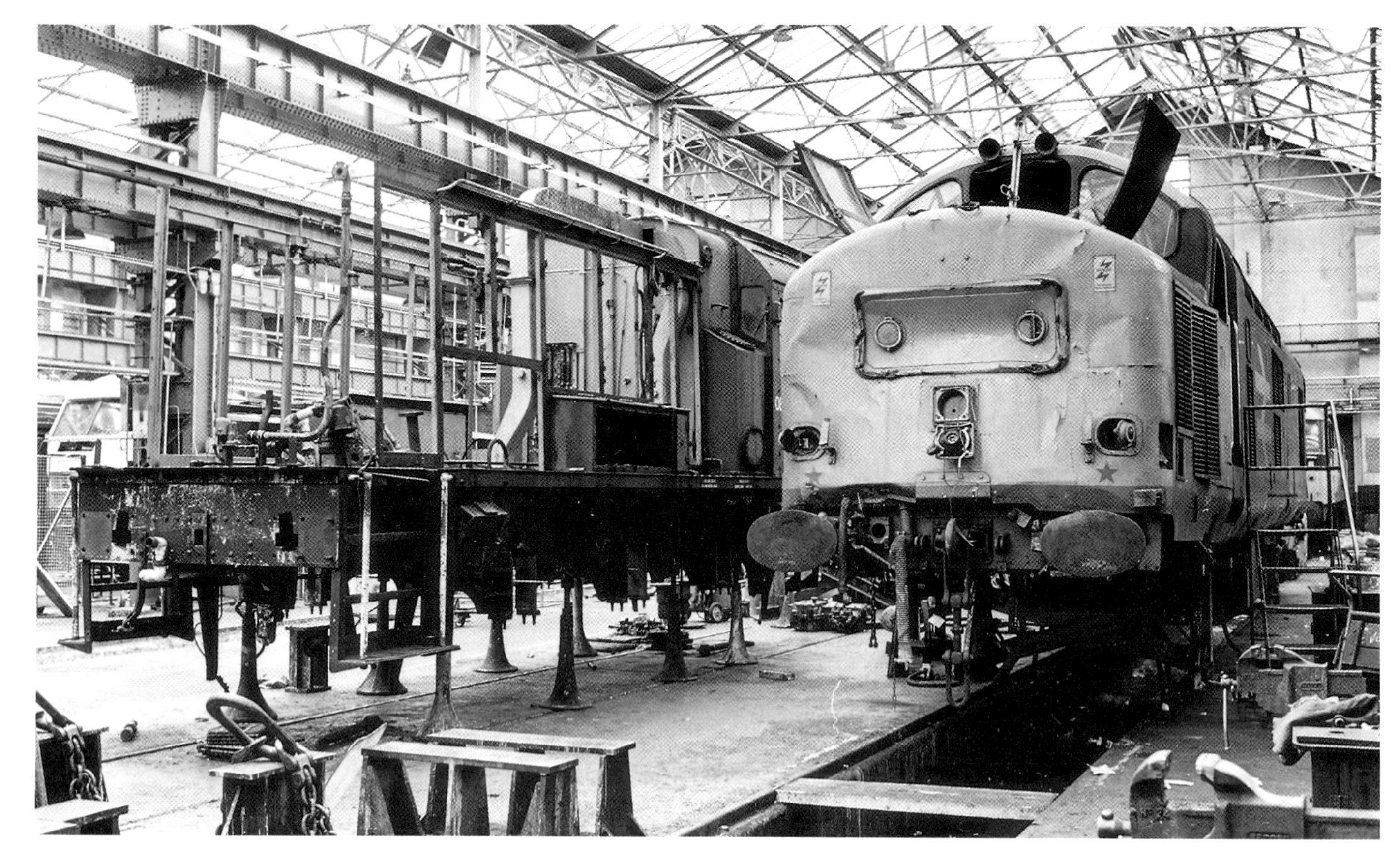

The acquisition by Railfreight of various locomotive types has been more readily identified in 1988 by the application of the sector's distinctive double-grey livery, repaints having been performed to various Class 08s, 26s, 31s, 33s, 37s, 47s, 56s, 58s and 86/5s.During February Class 47/4 No. 47599 was released from BREL Crewe in Railfreight colours, this being followed by several others during the year. One member of the Class 37/4 sub-class has also emerged in the new Railfreight livery.

For a short period during the year the Railfreight Train Ferry Shunting pool locomotives Nos. 33203/5/6 were deemed to become Class 33/ 3 and renumbered 33301-3, however, only one locomotive, No. 33302, bore its new identity for a few weeks only during the autumn.

The Isle of Wight saw a further addition to stock in 1988 when Class 03 No. 03179 was transferred to the Island's Civil Engineering fleet in May, being transported to Ryde on 30th June. By December the locomotive had been rebuilt with reduced height cab and repainted in Network South-East livery.

At a time when blue livery is fastly becoming a thing of the past it is interesting to record that during May Class 73/0 No. 73001 was repainted into standard rail blue from revised blue with wrap-round yellow ends, after receiving a classified overhaul at BRML Eastleigh. The reason for this apparent change of policy being due to the locomotive's Departmental sector ownership.

Also on the Class 73 scene February saw the formation of a new sub-class – 73/2, when 12 members of the 73/1 fleet were redesignated as Class 73/2, and renumbered 73201–12. The reason – their allocation to the InterCity–Victoria Gatwick service. Although at first it was considered likely that the diesel engines would be isolated, this alteration was not made.

The year saw the usual high number of locomotive namings and re-namings (see list at back of book) and an increase in locomotive de-namings. For the majority standard style nameplates were fitted to locomotives and new style brushed aluminium to High Speed Train powercars and Class 90 locomotives.

▲With the sale of BREL to the private sector looming the group have purchased some Class 08 locomotives from the BRB, enabling them to perform shunting duties without the expense of hiring locomotives and drivers. The machine purchased for BREL Crewe No. 08470 was given classified attention at Crewe in spring 1988, and is seen here in the main shop alongside Class 37 No.37671. The previous repair effected on No. 08470 was in December 1979 at BREL Swindon.
Colin J Marsden

▼1988 saw the adoption of miniature numbers for reliveried InterCity locomotives, the numbers being applied at sole bar level by the driver's cab door position.The numbers being so small were only readable when locomotives were stationary. Class 86/2 No. 86229 shows the revised number style. At the end of 1988 numbers twice the size were authorised for application, following complaints from the operating staff.
Michael J. Collins

▲Following classified attention at BRML Doncaster in the early part of the year, Class 47/9 No. 47901 was outshopped in Railfreight Construction livery. Due to a number of technical problems with its power unit/alternator the locomotive's performance back on the WR was poor and the locomotive returned to Doncaster for attention, where it is seen in this November view. *Brian Morrison*

►Vic Berry of Leicester, usually known for scrapping locomotives and stock, signed a contract during 1988 to repaint a batch of 9 Class 31 locomotives for Railfreight. The first locomotive to be completed was No. 31275 in early October, seen here in the works yard coupled to a Mark 2 coach also repainted by Berry's. *John Stretton*

▼To many people, the painting of e.t.h.-fitted mixed traffic locos in Railfreight livery and the imposition of a 75 mph speed restriction is rather strange, as these locomotives can sometimes be required for use on passenger services in emergency. No. 47600 sporting the last three digits of its number on the front end is illustrated, painted in Railfreight Speedlink livery. *Michael J. Collins*

LIVERY AND DESIGN

The application of the latest style Inter-City livery to locomotives continued during the year with HST power cars, Class 37, 47, 86, 87, 90 and 91 locomotives being treated.

Class 37 locomotives received the basic livery, the bodyside design not allowing room for the logo. Class 47, 86 and 87 locomotives received the new style with italicised INTERCITY logo. Only HST power cars, Class 90 and 91 locomotives received the full livery with the lower part of the body painted white instead of grey with 'swallow' motif alongside the logo. Hauled stock would receive the stylised INTERCITY logo upon repaint.

Towards the end of the year the British Rail design panel took the decision to dispense with the small stock numbers applied to locomotives and use standard size numerals. This decision was welcomed by enthusiasts but even more so by British Rail's own operating staff. Coaching stock continued to receive small numbers.

A number of repaints of Class 08 locomotives into sector colours took place during 1988. The top view by M.J. Collins shows No. 08631 painted in Network SouthEast livery for shunting duties at Cambridge, whilst the centre photograph by Hugh Ballantyne shows No. 08644 painted in InterCity colours. It is interesting to note that No. 08644 carries the IC sector 'swallow' motif, which is supposed to only be applied to locomotives able to travel at 100 mph or above! The Network SouthEast locomotive No. 08631 carries the official style name 'EAGLE C.U.R.C.' bestowed on the locomotive by the Cambridge University Railway Society.

▼During August one of Eastfield's Class 37/4s owned by the InterCity Charter sub-sector was painted in InterCity livery, but without the logo. No. 37401 *Mary Queen of Scots* is seen at Tyndrum Lower on 23rd September, at the head of the 12.04 Glasgow Queen Street–Oban service.
A.O. Wynn

COACHING STOCK

LOCOMOTIVE-HAULED STOCK

No new locomotive-hauled passenger coaches were completed during 1988, although the bodies for the new build of Mark 4 coaches were under construction later in the year at BREL's Derby Carriage Works under sub-contract for their builders, Metro-Cammell. There were, however, some new non-passenger-carrying coaching stock vehicles completed, these being the first of the Mark 3 driving van trailers for the West Coast Main Line. Strictly speaking, the official description does not accord with normal hauled stock practice, as all hauled coaching stock vehicles are trailers and they should really have been described as DBG (driving gangwayed brake vehicle). However, we are now stuck with the inconsistent term 'driving van trailer', and the vehicles themselves are stencilled DVT. The design of these vehicles, is very pleasing and resembles a Class 90 locomotive, so much so that this has fooled a few younger enthusiasts who have written to us to enquire why the Class 82 locomotives are missing from the 'Motive Power Pocket Book'! The DVTs have been built to improve the economics of operating the West Coast Main Line (WCML). Their main benefits are:

(1) Reduced turnround time at termini.
(2) Elimination of the need for a turnover locomotive at terminal stations, e.g. Euston, Manchester, Liverpool and Glasgow.
(3) Reduction in numbers of shunting staff.

As new locomotives (Class 90) were being built for WCML services, the introduction of DVTs meant that fewer locos needed to be ordered.

▼Jane E.Clarke, Project Engineer for the Mark 3 DVT project shows off her design at Derby Carriage Works in December. *Peter Fox*

An important conversion during 1988 was that of 22 Mark 2F open firsts to restaurant buffet firsts (RFB). Numbers were allocated in the 1200 series. These were the first production-series Mark 2 buffets and appeared 24 years after the first Mark 2 coach was delivered in 1964! Another interesting conversion was that of Mark 1 RB 1693 to RK 80041 for use in the InterCity charter fleet based at Bounds Green (London). RKs are unique in that they have passenger vehicle design codes, but are numbered in the non-passenger series. The conversion of various types of Mark 3 vehicle to RFM continued, and these gradually entered service on the WCML.

The new influx of catering vehicles enabled the withdrawal of the last of the 15XX series RKBs, which were also the last remaining hauled coaches built by Cravens of Sheffield. All RBs in the 17XX series were also withdrawn. These were of the same type as the remaining vehicles in the 16XX series, but contained blue asbestos. Withdrawals of ordinary Mark 1 coaches continued, and included BSK 34925, the last passenger coach built by Charles Roberts of Wakefield. The ex-Charles Roberts Works is now owned by Procor and is back in the railway coach business, albeit as sub-contractor for Metro-Cammell, building bodies for Class 156 DMUs. In addition to Mark 1s, many early Mark 2 vehicles were also withdrawn, including 21 Mark 2 TSOs and 5 FKs which had blue asbestos insulation. Most coaches withdrawn were 100 mph vehicles, but by the end of the year there were still 64 90 mph passenger vehicles in capital stock.

▼A Mark 4 coach body under construction at Derby Carriage Works in December. *Peter Fox*

▲The first completed Mark 3 DVT No. 82101 poses in Derby Carriage Works Yard. *Peter Fox*

◄The Mark 3 sleeping cars allocated to Bounds Green for the InterCity charter fleet have been painted in a special variant of the new InterCity livery. The word 'Sleeper' is painted on the side, and the roof is painted white. No. 10724 was photographed at Bounds Green on 27th February.
Michael J. Collins

►22 RFBs were converted during 1988 from Mark 2F FOs and went into service on West Coast Main Line and Cross-Country services. This photograph shows No. 1206, in the new style InterCity livery.
Peter Fox

▼The rather cramped bar area of an RFB showing the kitchen with microwave cooking facilities. *Peter Fox*

▼►The saloon at the kitchen end. The door in the centre leads to the kitchen. On the right can be seen the payphone booth. *Peter Fox*

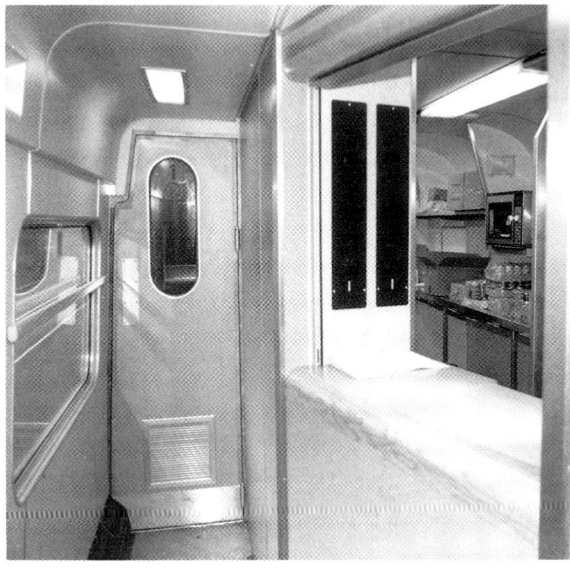

◄An unusual coach was finished by BREL Derby Carriage Works during 1988. This was a special saloon for President Bongo of the Gabon. It carries the logo of the state railway company, OCTRA which stands for 'Office du Chemin de Fer Transgabonais'. *Peter Fox*

▼Part of the interior of the saloon. The other end is furnished with modern reclining chairs and has video, television and projection facilities. *Peter Fox*

►The unusual (for 1988) design of toilet compartment, based on a design for Queen Victoria!
Peter Fox

DIESEL MULTIPLE UNITS

To provide higher capacity diesel unit stock principally for Chester based duties, five of Derby's Class 150/1 units Nos. 150 141-3/6/7 were augmented to 3-car formation in May by placing a Class 150/2 coach between the original vehicles. No renumbering was effected and the sets may be reformed again at a later date.

The new Class 155/156 Super Sprinter units came on stream, again not without problems. By the beginning of 1988 the Class 155 had completed its 'type-testing' at the Derby M&EE Department and the first Class 156 had arrived at the Engineering Development Unit. The Class 156 was officially launched at a special press call at Norwich on 12 January. Both types, after carrying out driver/artisan training, commenced regular service in May (see Provincial section). It is unfortunate to record that the entire fleet of Class 155 Leyland Sprinters were removed from service from 16th December due to serious door problems. This shortage resulted in the use of either loco-hauled stock formations or borrowed DMUs for services, with the knock-on effect being felt throughout the country.

Due to major technical problems with the West Yorkshire PTE Class 141 fleet and their incompatibility with other air-braked DMUs remedial action was authorised and commenced in 1988. The work involved, called 're-working' by BR, was almost a total refurbishment of the mechanical parts, with units being moved to Andrew Barclay's works at Kilmarnock for attention. Apart from fully overhauling all technical equipment the most noticeable external alteration was the removal of the nose-and body-mounted air pipes and control jumpers and the replacement of Tightlock couplers with the BSI type incorporating physical, electrical and air connections. Concurrent with their re-working the Class 141s were out-shopped in the latest West Yorkshire PTE livery of cream and red. The first unit to be dealt with was No. 141 109 which was returned to BR in June.

Again, due to gear box failures a substantial number of Class 142 units were stored out of use during 1988. In an attempt to improve the position the EDU of the Railway Technical Centre carried out a number of equipment monitoring programmes during the early months of the year, and this resulted in the re-equipping of some units with a Voith hydraulic transmission. A similar low availability problem attributable to transmission faults befell the Class 143 units; this has also been remedied by a programme of replacement with Voith hydraulic units, work being effected by RFS Engineering of Doncaster, at a cost of some £1.7 m.

The West Yorkshire PTE Class 144 units were in the news during the spring, when 10 sets, Nos. 144 014–023, were augmented to 3-car units by the addition of a Motor Second (MS), bodies being constructed by Walter Alexander and married to BREL (1988) Ltd. underframes at Derby Litchurch Lane. West Yorkshire PTE also took delivery of seven Class 155 units later in the year.

◀The private sector works of Andrew Barclay won the contract to 're-work' the Class 141 'railbus' fleet during 1988. This work included the virtual refurbishing of all parts, as well as fitting BSI couplings in place of the previous 'tightlock' type, which required air/control jumpers to be mounted on the vehicles nose end. Awaiting entry to the Kilmarnock plant on 17th March are sets 141 001/013.
Maxwell H. Fowler

▼During the early months of 1988 an increasing number of Class 142 units were stored because of transmission faults. One of the main storage locations was Crewe carriage shed, where on 12th February Nos. 142 032/002/007/008/010/029/045 were recorded. *Brian Morrison*

▲An interesting reformation of some Sprinter Class 150/1 units were effected in May when 5 sets were augmented with a Class 150/2 car coupled in the centre. The reforming was carried out at Derby, and the use of a Class 150/2 vehicle enabled access throughout the train. Aesthetically the reforming looked a mess with the middle car having different body lines and in most cases a different livery. On 23rd July, No. 150 141 passes Sutton Bridge Junction with the 10.07 Llandovery–Crewe service, the middle car being 57253 from set No. 150 253. *John Tuffs*

►Newly strengthened to three cars, WYPTE-liveried unit No. 144 023 arrives at Ilkley with the 17.20 from Bradford Forster Square on 4th April. *A.J. Woof*

▼Class 104 2-car unit 53466/53511 found its way to Tyseley during 1988. Still in all blue livery, it is seen at Leamington with a Stratford-on-Avon service. *John B. Gosling*

▲SR diesel-electric multiple units also appeared in Network SouthEast livery for the first time this year. Class 205 '3H' unit 205 012 rumbles through pleasant countryside near Ham Street with the 15.04 Ashford–Hastings service on 3rd August. The number has been repositioned centrally below the headcode panel, receiving the author's booby prize for probably the most unattractive position yet devised. *Brian Morrison*

ELECTRIC MULTIPLE UNITS

During the course of 1988, three new classes of EMU stock were placed in service, not without problems. From the commencement of the 1988 summer timetable in May Class 319 EMUs entered service on the Network SouthEast 'Thameslink' line, units being allocated to Selhurst. The May service commenced with only 75% of the fleet available, but by the year end all 60 sets had been commissioned. Also scheduled to enter service in May, again for Network SouthEast, were the Class 442 'Wessex Electric' units. However, due to late delivery by BREL (owing to protracted delivery of components), very few sets were introduced in the summer timetable. During the summer months, as more units were commissioned at Bournemouth, these were slotted into diagrams, but a full Class 442 service was not attempted until October, even at the year end many substitute formations were still to be found. One of the major problems with the Class 442 stock was with plug doors, which at first had a tendency to open at high speed as air pressure caused suction, and latterly with electrical problems. This culminated in the passenger door control buttons being disconnected for a period.

Although not diagrammed for passenger service in 1988 the first of 71 Class 321 EMUs No. 321 301 for the NSE–Anglia services was handed over from BREL to Network SouthEast sector director Chris Green at York on 15th September. Initial testing and proving of units was carried out between Doncaster and Peterborough.

The redundant Class 210 DMU stock which had been stored at the Railway Technical Centre, Derby, for many months, came into the news during the summer when 4 vehicles, Nos. 60300/01, 60400/01, were rebuilt by the Engineering Development Unit as a test bed for 3-phase motors of a similar type to those projected for the new 'Networker' units. After the stock was transferred to the Southern on 20th June 1988, cars Nos. 60300/01, 60401 were marshalled with car Nos. 71733 from Class 455/9 No. 5920, and classified as No. 457 001. The new Class 457 was allocated to Strawberry Hill from where it carried out equipment testing prior to receiving internal alterations at Selhurst before entering public service at the year end. To operate alongside unit 7001 the 3 remaining vehicles of 455/9 No. 5920 were coupled with Class 210 vehicle No. 60400. Both units carry the legend 'Traction Development for the 1990s' on their bodysides. All former Class 210 vehicles now operating as EMUs have had their numbers altered by the addition of 7,000.

A start was made towards the end of 1988 to replace the 1927 Isle of Wight passenger stock when several London Transport 1938 tube vehicles were purchased for conversion. During October/November several train loads of vehicles were transferred to the Southern Region at Strawberry Hill, where a final selection of vehicles was made. In early 1989 these were scheduled for transfer to BRML Eastleigh to be rebuilt. The new stock is scheduled to enter service for the 1989 summer timetable.

Following a fatal attack on a female passenger travelling in compartment stock on the Network SouthEast the decision was taken to re-form stock – where practicable – to eliminate compartments from off-peak services, and additionally identify all compartment type vehicles by a red roof band. On the SR 32 4EPB (Class 415) units were re-formed to provide 'peak hour' sets, each having 2 Trailer Second compartment vehicles. Units so treated were reclassified 415/5 and renumbered in the 5501–32 series.

◄Out-shopped from BRML Wolverton, the first Class 310/1 EMU and the first of the type to be painted into Provincial Sector colours is posed for the camera outside the Works on 31st August. The 'Midline' logo which should have been included is missing at this stage and renumbering to 310 101 has yet to take place. *Brian Morrison*

►After many months laying dormant in the Railway Technical Centre Yard at Derby, some of the Class 210 stock was returned to service in 1988, as an EMU! To enable testing of equipment for the 'Networker' series of stock, including 3-phase traction motors and advanced control equipment. This was installed on 4 vehicles by the Engineering Development Unit, Derby. Coach 60300 (67300) is seen under repair at Derby on 19th May. *Colin J. Marsden*

►A further renumbering of Network SouthEast 4 EPB stock occurred in the summer; 32 units operating on the South East section were reformed with 2 compartment trailer vehicles, and were diagrammed for use only in the peak period; this followed an attack on a passenger who was in a compartment in the off-peak period when few passengers were travelling. The new number range allocated was 5501-32, and in addition to this a wide red band had been applied at cant rail height on the side of the compartment vehicles. Set No. 5517 is illustrated. *Brian Morrison*

►In September Anglia Region completed a new Sandite and Brakedown train at Ilford rebuilt from redundant Class 302 stock. The new 'unit' was renumbered 302 996 and painted in cargo green and biscuit with a black band. The set was outshopped from Ilford 'B' shop on 26th September, the day this photograph was taken. *Brian Morrison*

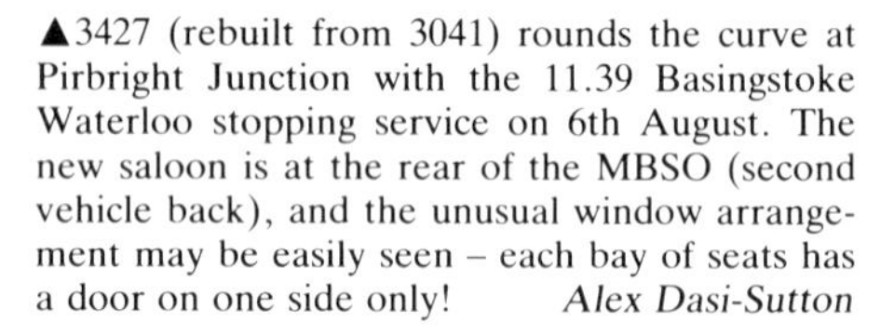

▲3427 (rebuilt from 3041) rounds the curve at Pirbright Junction with the 11.39 Basingstoke Waterloo stopping service on 6th August. The new saloon is at the rear of the MBSO (second vehicle back), and the unusual window arrangement may be easily seen – each bay of seats has a door on one side only! *Alex Dasi-Sutton*

◄After many rumours and counter-rumours, BR finally acknowledged that it was to replace the venerable ex-London Transport 'standard' tube stock running on the Isle of Wight, the oldest of which dates from 1926. The 'new' stock going to the island has again been bought from LUL, this time being vehicles of 1938 tube stock. These had been retained in use until earlier in 1988 on the Northern Line, since when they had been stored at West Ruislip Depot, where they unfortunately received the attentions of graffiti vandals. The first delivery of seven cars to Strawberry Hill took place on Friday 14th October, when 33117 was seen hauling the train at Kensington Olympia, running almost one hour ahead of booked time. The cars behind the loco are 11116 and 12087.
David Brown

◄Electric multiple unit stock has also been sold to Vic Berry's for disposal with examples of Southern, Eastern and Scottish Region stock being reported at the site. This illustration taken on 28th February shows 7 vehicles of former Class 303/311 Trans-Clyde units in a stockpile.
Paul Biggs

DEPARTMENTAL STOCK

Departmental numbers ADB 977568–KDB 977622 were allocated in 1988, these numbers encompassing a mixture of test train coaches, sandite coaches, instruction coaches, brake force runners, route learning units, tractor units and S&T staff coaches. Surprisingly, no less than sixteen of the fifty-five coaches allocated for departmental use were Mark 2 coaches. Class 90 test train coaches ADB 977568–77/95 were formerly 5504/14/35/43/5/55/9/71/83, 9470 and 13573 respectively whilst earmarked for the Doncaster BRML test train and allocated numbers ADB 977596/7 and ADB 977616 were 13471, 6403 and 13468 respectively. 6402 became brake force runner DB 977589, whilst 17033 became S&T staff coach KDB 977591. The most significant conversion was the completion at Cardiff Cathays CWMD of ultrasonic test train coaches DB 977391/2, formerly Class 101 Metro-Cammell power cars 51433 and 53167.

Of those departmental coaches or vans condemned or scrapped in 1988, TDS 70166 attracted the most interest. TDS 70166 was formerly South East and Chatham Railway PMV S 2001 S, built at Ashford in 1922. TDS 70166 had been taken into departmental stock in December 1962 as a generator van for one of the 'secret' mobile emergency control trains. These were trains kept at strategic locations throughout British Rail, which could be used as headquarters in the event of war. TDS 70166 was kept out of sight in the old steam shed at Tunbridge Wells West, until the decision to disband these trains was taken in 1979. TDS 70166 was then stored first at Bricklayers Arms and later Ashford until in 1988 the decision was taken to condemn it at Hoo Junction.

For most of 1988 former prototype HST Buffet Car No. W 40500 was undergoing a major refit in the R&D Division Engineering Test Hall, due to emerge in spring 1989 as a high speed brake development coach. Also on the prototype HST front, power car No. RDB 975813 was rescued from BREL Derby Locomotive Works and taken over by Research for a series of trials on the Old Dalby test track involving stability after hitting objects on the track, by the end of 1988 the vehicle was again redundant.

A new Severn Tunnel emergency train was completed in January by Cardiff Cathays Carriage & Wagon depot, formed of emergency casualty coach – TDB 977526, water tanker TDB 999098, generator coach TDB 904708 and inspection vehicle TDB 905093.

The new train was based at Sudbrook Sidings with former Class 09 No. 97806 (09017).

▲TDS 70166, one of only a very small number of pre-grouping vehicles still extant on BR in 1988, is seen on 30th April at Hoo Junction awaiting for disposal through the Director of Procurement at Derby. *Bob Wallace*

►Although the allocation of departmental number DB 977391 was made in 1986, the conversion of this vehicle was not completed until 1988 and this photograph shows DB 977391 at Cardiff Cathays on 18th May just after the completion of its conversion from a Class 101 Metro Cammell power car to the staff, dormitory and generator coach of an ultrasonic test train. *Deryck Lewis*

►Looking rather bedraggled, one of the prototype HST power cars (43001), now RDB 975813, entered service with the Research division for a short period in 1988, when experiments into hitting track objects were conducted. The 'power car' is now all but a shell, and it is expected to be sold for scrap. *Colin J. Marsden*

TECHNOLOGY

ELECTRIFICATION

The extension of third-rail electric services from Bournemouth to Weymouth is covered under 'Network SouthEast'. A fill-in scheme which extended the 25 kV from Royston to Cambridge ended the regular changing of trains at Royston for many commuters. The most important scheme, however, was the East Coast Main Line electrification, which was extended as far as Leeds. In this connection, a new electrification fixed equipment depot and control room was opened at Doncaster, adjacent to the motive power depot. It was opened by local MP Harold Walker on 29th April. Maintenance crews based at the depot will cover the 115 route miles of overhead line equipment from Newark to Thirsk and Leeds, but the power control room will monitor the 25 kV supply as far north as Chathill. The power supply is computer-controlled, and the traditional control panels with track diagrams and lights have given to VDUs. Twenty eight remote switching stations are monitored, including eight feeder stations where power is taken from the CEGB and transformed to the required 25 kV.

SPECIAL PLANT

Following the successful trials in 1987 of the Plasser and Theurer self-propelled Dynamic Track Stabiliser DR 72201 and the same company's 09–32 CSM Tamper/Liner DR 73101, BR took delivery in 1988 of DR 72202–13 and DR 73102/3/5, the ER DR 72204/5/8, the WR DR 72203/9, DR 73104/6, the ScR DR 72206 and DR 73107, the SR DR 72211/2 and the Anglia Region DR 72213. As InterCity had agreed to finance the purchase of DR 72202–10, whilst Network SouthEast had purchased DR 72211–3, each machine was emblazoned with the name of the purchasing sector.

All these machines were manufactured in Austria and DR 73102s first attempt to reach Dover via the Dunkerque ferry ended in it being damaged in an accident in Germany and having to be returned to Linz for rebuilding. The two other machines purchased as part of the same order were 08–16/90 DR 73501 and 08–275 DR 73903. The purchase of 08–16/90 DR 73501 is of particular interest in that it is widely believed that two-axle machines will become increasingly popular as lightweight machines are, of course, much cheaper.

In addition to the twenty machines detailed above, Plasser and Theurer also supplied to BR nine General Purpose Trams DR 98213–21. The other major purchase of on-track plant in 1988 was the delivery from Permaquip of sixteen High Capacity Overhead Work Trolleys, these mainly being allocated to principle OHLM depots on the ECML and WCML.

1988 saw the end of an era which had begun over one hundred years earlier. To be precise on 1st June the boiler certificate on Ransomes and Rapier steam breakdown crane ADRR 95210 finally ran out. ADRR 95210 had been built in 1940 and had a 45-ton lifting capacity and following use at a variety of Southern Region locations, it was transferred to Stewarts Lane and to its place in railway history as the last active steam breakdown crane on BR.

1988 was expected to see the demise of the last examples of the Matisa track-recording trolleys, as it had been anticipated that the Class 150 Track Recording Unit would render the small fleet of survivors redundant. However, a number of these trolleys will continue to be programmed for work in 1989.

▲A retrograde step. During 1988, the ITV teletext service, Oracle, ceased to carry BR information because of lack of adequate information from BR. The BBC service, CEEFAX, continued to carry BR news, but it is the author's opinion that the service leaves much to be desired. *Peter Fox*

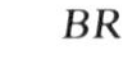

▼The new Electrification depot at Doncaster. *BR*

▲The interior of the new o.h.l.e. control room at Doncaster showing the VDUs used for monitoring the power supply. *Steve Chapman*

▼Transition at Northallerton. The 14.30 Edinburgh–King's Cross HST, with power cars 43074 and 43198, passes the 1939-built signal box and searchlight-type colour light signal on 19th August. The masts are in position for electrification, and the resignalling of the area was being undertaken. *Paul Shannon*

BR MISCELLANY

▲Organised by the Thanet area manager of Network SouthEast was a railway gala weekend on 3/4th September. One of the main attractions was preserved 'Deltic' No. D9000 Royal Scots Gray, which was moved to Margate from Stewarts Lane depot. The locomotive is seen stabled in the station displaying its Flying Scotsman headboard, slightly out of context for the south coast! *Brian Morrison*

▼The BR-owned 4SUB EMU was used on several tours during the year, often traversing tracks that were not usually frequented by the type when in regular service. In connection with the 'Thanet Rail Gala' held at Margate on 3rd/4th September the unit was used on a special shuttle between Margate and Ramsgate, entitled the 'Thanet Belle'. The special is seen approaching Broadstairs. *Brian Morrison*

►On 30th January, Pathfinder Tours' 'The Fellsman' worked from Taunton to Carlisle via Shap and returned via the Settle and Carlisle line and Leicester. Class 50s Nos. 50008 Thunderer and 50034 Furious head the train at Birkett Common, south of Kirkby Stephen, in miserable weather. On the 'Down' line is a Hertfordshire Railtours HST excursion on a St. Pancras–Carlisle–Newcastle–King's Cross circuit. *Hugh Ballantyne*

▼Following the repainting of Class 45 No. 45106 into green livery, it was requested for several special trains, one was Pathfinder Railtours' 'Wessex Adventurer' operated on 5th November from Manchester to Weymouth, including a trip over the rarely- traversed Fawley line. The resplendent locomotive and Mark 2 formation are seen departing from Southampton bound for Weymouth. *Alex Dasi-Sutton*

▲Five vehicles of BR's Gatwick Express stock was used on a special 'tour' on Sunday 2nd October, when it formed a LRT railtour from Wimbledon to Wimbledon via the 'widened' lines. Motive power was provided by LT battery locomotives Nos. 65 & 67 coupled one at each end of the stock. Whilst traversing the SR the locomotives had to use their battery power. The train is seen near Wimbledon with a Class 455 unit passing on the down main line.
Colin J Marsden

◄During the course of the year a number of railtours were operated using multiple unit stock, one which traversed some unusual track was on 30th April when the Southern Electric Group's 'Inner City Express 2' tour formed of green-liveried Class 203 No.203 001 and Network SouthEast-liveried Class 207 No. 207 002 operated around the suburban area as well as working into Fenchurch Street, Liverpool Street and King's Cross. The train is seen passing Shadwell en route for Fenchurch Street. *Alex Dasi-Sutton*

◄207 002 is seen at King's Cross on the same day flanked by Class 47 No. 47522 and HST power car No. 43085. *David Percival*

►The Pathfinder Tours special from Reading to Holyhead provided a 'first' on 17th July, when Class 47 No. 47238, and Class 45 No. 45012 powered the train along the Conwy Valley line, this being the first Class 45 ever to have visited the route. The train is seen passing Dolwydellan heading back to Llandudno Junction from where it is reversed and carried onto Holyhead. *Larry Goddard*

►Class 45/1 No. 45128 approaches Bidston from the Mersey Docks Harbour Board lines with the 'Mersey Docker' tour. The London Euston–Birkenhead tour ran on 20th February. *Les Nixon*

▼Resplendent in green livery, with small yellow warning ends, and just the No. D 200 on its bodyside the 'Green Goddess' is seen on 2nd April passing Bangor with the Hertfordshire Railtours' 'Tubular Belle' special from Euston to Holyhead. For this trip the Class 40 was used only between Crewe and Holyhead, with ac electric traction being provided under the wires. *A.J. Woof*

▲The CEGB usually hold a number of open days at their power stations each year, and if possible include BR in their displays. During 1988 these events were used for the naming ceremonies for several Railfreight Coal-sector locomotives. The open day held at Didcot on 16th June included the naming of Class 58 No. 58014 Didcot Power Station. The newly-named locomotive and GWR 28XX No. 3822 are seen in the yard. *Brian Morrison*

▼There have been few occasions when triple heading of a railtour has been permitted, however on 3rd September special dispensation was given for the running of the 'Coupled Crompton' tour organised by the Southern Electric Group and traversing various lines on the SR. Motive power was provided by one example of each Class 33 sub-class, Nos. 33209, 33051 Shakespeare Cliff and 33112 Templecombe. The train is seen departing from Gravesend en route from Grain to Margate. *David Brown*

▲One of the most unusual motive power formations to head a railtour in 1988 was on 8th May, when the Southern Electric Group's 'Flying Fourgon' tour of numerous Network SouthEast routes had Motor Luggage Vans (MLV) Nos. 9007/10 and a Gatwick Luggage Van No. 9109 providing the motive power for 4TCT set No. 8103 for part of the full day's tour. The train is seen passing Southerham Junction. *Chris Wilson*

►Denby Dale stages an occasional 'Pie Day', an ancient tradition in which the largest meat pie in the world is baked! A half-hourly service was provided on the Huddersfield–Sheffield (via Penistone and Barnsley) line and were all well-used. This line had been under threat of closure but is now entirely PTE-supported by WYPTE and SYPTE. *Peter Fox*

►On the 16th May Halewood station was opened. Funded by the Merseyside PTE it is, unusually for new stations, staffed. It has waiting rooms of brick construction on both platforms. A Class 108 set calls at Halewood (on a Hunt's Cross–Manchester Oxford Road working) on its first operational day.
Stephen J. Chapman

▼Class 37 No. 37428 David Lloyd George brings the ECS out of Abbey Foregate carriage sidings under the largest remaining GWR/WR signal gantry at Shrewsbury. This gantry was removed and cut up in October 1988. *Andrew Bannister*

▼►Further west, the end was in sight for the ex-GWR signalling at Dovey Junction in May 1988. This was the scene prior to track remodelling in preparation for the Cambrian Line radio signalling (RETB) scheme.
Andrew Bannister

►Another signalbox casualty of 1988 was Black Bank, situated on the Fens near Ely. The box was extant but internally derelict seven days after closure when photographed on 21st May.
Michael J. Collins

▲Class 91, InterCity's new flagship locomotive did not enter revenue-earning service during 1988 because of software 'bugs' coupled with excessive noise in the cab. 91004 is seen here at Stevenage propelling an up test train on 25th July. *David Percival*

▲The new Class 321 EMUs for East Anglia had a stylish appearance but were criticised for their lack of through gangways. 321 301 was photographed at Doncaster on 1st October. *John Augustson*

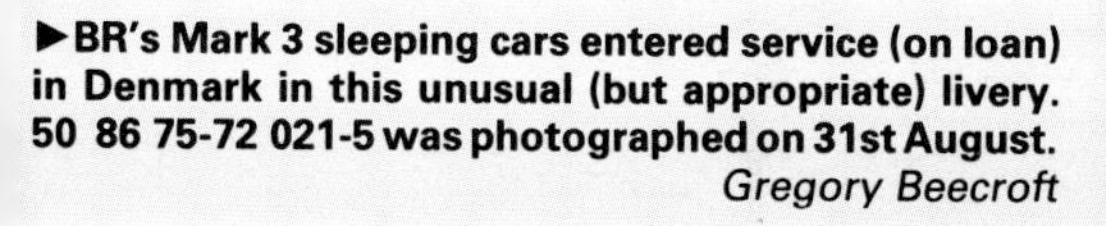

►BR's Mark 3 sleeping cars entered service (on loan) in Denmark in this unusual (but appropriate) livery. 50 86 75-72 021-5 was photographed on 31st August. *Gregory Beecroft*

▲The first Class 37 loco. D 6700 (alias 37350) was repainted in BR green livery for working railtours. It is seen approaching Worcester Shrub Hill with a train of Network SouthEast-liveried Mark 1 stock on 5th June with the Hertfordshire Railtours 'Coalville Cobbler'. *John Chalcraft*

◄The sole remaining Class 40 in BR stock No. 40122 (D 200) was given another coat of green paint before final preservation at the NRM. Unfortunately it was not possible to complete the job between tours, resulting in it having to work the Pathfinder Tours 'Pennine 40 Farewell' in light grey undercoat, here seen on 12th March at Euston! *Stephen Widdowson*

▼The National Railway Museum's Class 502 unit (M28361 and M29896) in LMS livery was once again in action on its old stamping ground on the Wirral Peninsula. The unit was drafted in to run alongside modern Class 508 units to provide a regular service between Rock Ferry and Hooton over the May Day Bank Holiday weekend as part of the Lever Bros. Port Sunlight centenary celebrations. The magnificent maroon livery of the unit catches the afternoon sunshine as it arrives at Spital en route to Hooton on 2nd May. *Les Nixon*

PRESERVATION

There can be little doubt that the preservation event of the year was the celebration run of *MALLARD* from Doncaster to Scarborough on 3rd July commemorating the 50th anniversary of its historic 126 mph dash down Stoke Bank. The crowds at Doncaster rivalled those at Ais Gill on the day the final 'official' BR steam-hauled 15 guinea special on 11th August 1968. Indeed the 20th anniversary of this event was celebrated in style by Class 8F No. 48151 hauling a special from Derby to Manchester; a somewhat less eventful trip than her inaugural run on 16th April when, on this newly-approved steam route, inferior firebars nearly made it a one-way rather than a return excursion.

Generally, 1988 was a year of optimism in railway preservation with numerous proposals to create new lines or to extend spheres of operation. These included – on the Isle of Wight Railway an extension from Haven Street to Smallbrook Junction – Kent and East Sussex Railway proposals to extend west to Northiam – the Strathspey Railway announced plans to ultimately reach Grantown on Spey – the Bluebell Railway commenced track laying on their extension to East Grinstead – the Llangollen Railway began work on the extension beyond Berwyn to the Deeside loop – the Gwili Railway extended its track a further 1½ miles – and the Pontypool and Blaenavon tabled plans to double its trackage to 1½ miles. Totally new projects included a proposal to reopen a 4 mile section of the former Banbury to Cheltenham line and a bid was announced to reopen the long abandoned ten mile Midhurst to Chichester link.

A preservation hiccup (or possibly a portent of the future for some in the preservation movement?) was the surprising decision by the Dart Valley Railway to discontinue using the BR facilities at Totnes station as from the end of the 1988 season. Declining receipts from passengers joining trains from this end of the line was the reason offered, although possibly the root cause was simply a result of inadequate promotion.

No review of the year would be complete without a mention of the LSWR 150th celebrations on the Southern Region. Over £20,000 was raised for charity at the very successful Woking event over the Spring Bank Holiday weekend whereas equally successful celebrations were held at Salisbury and Winchfield. The latter coinciding with the last steam runs to Yeovil under the direction of Salisbury Area Manager, Gerald Daniels. By way of total contrast the 150th year anniversary of the opening of the Sheffield and Rotherham Railway was allowed to pass without comment, nationally or locally.

The centenary of the Lever Bros. Port Sunlight margarine works was the focus of attention for enthusiasts in early May when no fewer than 31 special trains were operated over their private railway system by Jinty No. 7298 and Didcot based GW 2–6–2T No. 5572. Yet another notable event was the 125th anniversary of the Ffestiniog Railway.

Crewe Borough Council very generously agreed to partly finance the raising of some of the overhead catenary in the Crewe area to allow the return of steam to the town. BR responded by allowing *PRINCESS ELIZABETH* to cover new territory when it headed a circular tour from the town to Chester, Shrewsbury (reverse) and Whitchurch.

Share issues were seen to be the financial salvation of many private lines during the year with launches ranging from the modest target of £90,000 for the Gwili Railway extension through to an ambitious £500,000 for a new sound-proof boiler shop at the Bridgnorth site of the SVR. A similar amount was hoped for by the West Somerset Railway to purchase a 99 year lease of their 22 miles of line

▲It is always a pleasure to be able to report on preserved steam being permitted to run on 'new' BR lines. Partly compensating for the 1988 ban on steam operation over the Cambrian between Machynlleth, Aberystwyth and Pwllheli, *PRINCESS ELIZABETH* covered new territory when it was allowed to work a train out of Crewe for the first time since the official end of steam on BR. The circular tour was routed via Chester and Shrewsbury (reversal) followed by a further new track on the return leg to Crewe via Whitchurch. GW semaphores presented a pleasing 'olde worlde' counterpoint to 6201 as it sped past Weston Rhyn on 20th August. Operationally the 99 mile round trip seemed to be a sound proposition allowing two tours a day with 100% steam haulage from an easily accessible rail centre. The opening of the Crewe–Chester line heralds the promised return of steam to North Wales in 1989.
Brian Dobbs

▲The first Keighley and Worth Valley Railway diesel weekend was an undoubted success even if it did attract a few of the hooligan element of the younger enthusiast fraternity. The choice of motive power was impressive, bearing in mind that most of the locomotives had to be brought in from other preserved railways. Highlights included the opportunity to ride behind the double headed Deltics Nos. 55009/55019, Western No. D1041, Class 24 No. D5054 and home-based Class 25 No. D5209. Pictured here is *GORDON HIGHLANDER* leaving a characteristic Deltic trail of exhaust as it leaves Haworth for Keighley on the morning of 6th November. *Les Nixon*

from Somerset County Council.Other notable share issues were those of Peak Rail and the Midland Railway Centre, the latter's 'Midland Railway Enterprises plc' launch taking place on 1st June. Still on financial matters, quite staggering price increases of up to 20% were announced for travel on the ever popular Shakespeare Limited and the Pennines Limited. An incredible £1½ m support was pledged by various groups for the establishment of the Wales Railway Centre under the auspices of the Butetown Historic Railway Society at the former Taff Vale Bute Road terminus in Cardiff. Early in the year the complement of steam wrecks at this South Wales site was brought up to ten by further movements from nearby Barry.

CLAN LINE returned to the Settle and Carlisle route for the first time for ten years while *MALLARD* and 8F 48151 both enjoyed successful inaugural runs over the line. On a less happy note however David Ward announced that one-off steam specials would in future be positively discouraged. After a long period of on-off wrangles it was also finally announced that there would be no steam excursions on the Cambrian during the summer although on a more optimistic note it was revealed that advanced plans were being made to run steam excursions along the North Wales coast line in 1989.

Quite surprisingly, 1988 was the year when agreement was in prospect between the Dean Forest Railway and British Coal for the proposed movement of 3,000 tons of coal per week over a period of two years. Moreover, British Coal were to underwrite the relaying of the branch by flat bottomed track to an axle loading of 22 tons and the strengthening of appropriate bridges. Still on the freight scene, over in Kent on the Isle of Grain branch, West Country No. 34016 *BODMIN* was involved in the haulage of a ceremonial first freight train conveying concrete lining segments for the Channel Tunnel.

New images were promoted by both the Middleton and Bo'ness lines which in 1988 became known as the Middleton Park line and the Forth Valley Railway.

The BR closure in August of the Oakamoor branch south of Leek Brook Junction brought a new lease of life to the Cheddleton based North Staffordshire Railway Society who are now actively persuing the possibility of taking over all or part of the branch. Nearby the Peak Park Planning Board granted outline planning permission for the development

◄Most enthusiasts will tell you that the curtain came down on BR steam on 11th August 1968 but in reality the end came just over twenty years later, at the end of the summer season on the Vale of Rheidol. It was then agreed to sell the narrow gauge railway to the Brecon Mountain Railway. In this scene of the last summer on the Vale of Rheidol under BR management 2–6–2T No. 9 *PRINCE OF WALES* heads towards Devil's Bridge near Rheidol Falls. *Andrew Bannister*

▲Your editor makes no excuse for the inclusion of yet another picture of the celebrated A4 Pacific – after all it was *MALLARD's* year. Here it is at the head of one of the most colourful steam-hauled trains to travel on the main line of BR during 1988, the Post Office 'The Pennine Postal' charter which ran from Manchester (Victoria) to Scarborough. No. 4468, with two Post Office red TPOs coupled next to the engine, rounds the curve from Standedge tunnel towards Marsden on 10th May. *Gavin Morrison*

►If ever there was a railway event which would capture the imagination of both the public and the media it was certainly the 50th anniversary celebrations of *MALLARD's* record breaking run down Stoke Bank. Earlier in the year speculations were that No. 4468 might once again be allowed over the famed stretch of track between Peterborough and Grantham but in the event steam haulage was restricted to a run from Doncaster to York and Scarborough. Half a century on, but on the precise day of the famous event, 3rd July, unbelievable crowds gathered at Doncaster to see what is arguably the most famous steam locomotive in the world. The car park at the north end of the Doncaster station was clearly the favoured vantage point; indeed here it looks to be in danger of imminent collapse! *Gavin Morrison*

of the proposed Peak Rail Matlock–Buxton line. Further south BR agreed in principle to a proposal that the Chorley station and Wallingford might run into a bay platform at Cholsey station. Agreement was also reached for the sale of BR's last steam railway, The Vale of Rheidol, to the Brecon Mountain Railway.

All credit must go to those societies who achieved major objectives during the year. Of particular note was the first steam run on the Cholsey and Wallingford and the first run of a steam-hauled passenger train to Harman's Cross on the Swanage Railway on 3rd December. Over in East Anglia the North Norfolk Railway opened their line through to Holt.

Significant structures on the move during the year included the transfer of the turntable from Mold Junction to Peak Rail Buxton. The first moves were also made to move the famous Garsdale turntable to Keighley. The Midland Railway signal box at Kettering was moved to Butterley where it will be used to control train movements at Swanwick. Yet another large 62 lever box was installed at Kidderminster on the SVR. Ingrow station on the KWVR, a magnificent reconstruction of Foulridge station, was formally opened on 6th March when visiting Class 5700 pannier tank No. 7752 called with the first passenger train. A similar move was also in prospect in the south when part of the redundant LSWR station at Dorchester South was donated to the Swanage Railway. Sadly, 1988 was also a year of personality clashes and one-man takeover bids. The problems on the North Norfolk Railway were happily resolved but animosity continued to be the order of the day between

Mid-Hants volunteers and millionaire Glyn Evans.

MUSEUMS

A significant development was the Post Office-sponsored establishment of a permanent Mail by Rail exhibition at the National Railway Museum. An event which coincided with the 150th anniversary of the first travelling post office on the Grand Junction Railway.

Still on museum matters the NRM Class J52 0–6–0ST was moved to Hull for restoration work. Another notable publicity event was the cosmetic transformation of A4 *BITTERN* to fully valanced single chimneyed No. 2509 *SILVER LINK* in pre-war grey livery. The work was carried out at the works of ICI Wilton before movement to the NRM at York. Meanwhile the ever popular *DUCHESS OF HAMILTON* was finally purchased by the NRM and was the subject of a £50,000 appeal to return it to main line running order.

On the diesel front the extended BR life of NRM's D200 finally came to a glorious end when she worked a final special from Liverpool Street to York on 16th April. Sad news however from East Anglia where the owners of the Wolferton station museum declared that closure was inevitable at the end of the season unless approaches to the Royal Family allowed the erection of signposts on the nearby A149 trunk road. The Royal Saloon, retired from service in 1977, was transferred from NRM York to the Kelvin Hall museum in Glasgow. The North Shields Land Transport Museum received 03078 from Gateshead in May. In Cheshire the preserved 2-car Class 502 EMU retired to the Wirral Museum exactly 50 years after the electrification was inaugurated. Sesquicentennial celebrations of the LNWR was the excuse for jamborees at the Birmingham Railway Museum on 4th September when an impressive selection of power included the Rocket replica and cosmetically restored LNWR 1921 built 0–8–0 No. 9395. At Birmingham a decision was taken to set up a separate division 'Vintage Trains Ltd.' specifically to market railtours. The Midland Railway Centre formally opened their museum and exhibition site at Swanwick on 30th May.

DIESELS AND ELECTRICS

The year saw the end of Class 40 and 45 diesels in BR service. In addition to D200 the future seems assured for Class 40s Nos. 40012, 40013, 40018 and 40135 while No. 45135 was another 'Peak' to be saved by Michael Jacob from the scrap merchant's torch. The latter will eventually be transferred to the Matlock site of Peak Rail. Seemingly all preservation groups recognised the potential value of 'Rats' as motive power, for at one time it looked as though every system was determined to acquire at least one representative. The popularity of diesel weekends gained momentum with highly successful first time events at Llangollen, the East Lancashire and the Keighley and Worth

THE AUSTRALIAN CONNECTION

▲In an enterprising move Gresley Pacific *FLYING SCOTSMAN* commenced another bout of globetrotting when it left the UK to participate in the Australian Bicentennial celebrations. Here it stands in the Freightliner terminal of Tilbury Docks on 10th September awaiting shipment on the following day. *Mike Collins*

◄By October the A3 was already in revenue-earning service downunder and here it is seen leaving Melbourne (Spencer Street) station with an excursion for Seymour. Judging by the dull light it looks as though some of our indifferent 1988 summer weather was exported in the tender of 4472! *Harold Nave*

▲Class 5 No. 44932 made a welcome return to main line duty on 15th October when it was rostered to work the 'Mancunian' excursion from Derby to Manchester Victoria. The locomotive put in an indifferent performance and was brought to a stand in Marple tunnel on the return leg although even in the heyday of steam eleven coaches would have been considered to be a demanding task for a Class 5 on this difficult Trans-Pennine route. Complete with British Railways 1948-style lettering on the tender and a 17A Derby shed plate it is seen here struggling to get the train on the move from Edale station on the outward leg.

Les Nixon

◄One of the Midland Railway Trust's footplate staff holds one of 48151's half-melted firebars after the arrival of the 'Mancunian' at Manchester Victoria on 16th April. *Peter Fox*

►No. 48151 was chosen to work the train which celebrated the 20th anniversary of the end of steam traction on BR. Although the S & C would have been the obvious route, the 8F worked a return train from Derby through the Hope Valley to Manchester Victoria. 11th August 1968 was a beautiful sunny day in complete contrast to the same day twenty years on, as can be seen in this somewhat dismal picture of the train on the return leg ascending Miles Platting bank. Note the diesel providing rear end banking assistance. *Hugh Ballantyne*

▲'How time flies' is a well worn cliche but your editor was surprised to find that almost ten years had passed since *CLAN LINE* was last to work on the Settle and Carlisle line. Complete with the then single surviving operational *ETHEL* No. 3, the well travelled Bulleid Pacific was pictured climbing through Horton in Ribblesdale on 10th December. *Les Nixon*

Valley Railways. At Bury no fewer than four diesels, Nos. 25054, 25909, D7076 and D9531 made their maiden preservation runs. At Keighley receipts during their November weekend were more than sufficient to cover the not inconsiderable movement costs of 'foreign' power. In past years similar events have had BR locos in attendance to provide an interesting counterpoint, a practice which came to an end in 1988. Inadequate insurance cover was the official reason proferred by British Rail. Nevertheless earlier in the year Classes 156, 20, 31, 37/4 and 59 were in action on the Severn Valley although the sole BR representative at Keighley was a maroon-liveried WYPTE refurbished Class 141/1 unit. At long last a Western returned to their old south western haunts when D1048 moved from Southport to the Bodmin & Wenford Railway. *ELECTRA*, the former Woodhead Class EM2, was returned to Brunswick green and was noted at various locations in the south before movement to Hammerton Street, Bradford.

One of the more interesting diesel events of the year was the reappearance of Keighley's Class 25 No. 25059 on the main line when it was given permission to rescue failed Tyseley Jubilee *KOLHAPUR*. In contrast misfortune was the order of the day for Deltic No. 55009 on 30th May when it was seriously damaged by fire while working on the NYMR.

STEAM:

The expiry of boiler certificates brought the usual crop of last runs of several well known steamers; the most famous including *CITY OF WELLS* and *EVENING STAR*. Other steam retirements from main line service included *CLUN CASTLE* and *MALLARD*. Entering main line service were Class 5 44932, and 2–6–4T No. 80080; the latter making a rare tank engine foray on to main line duties when it worked both Nottingham–Derby–Matlock and Salisbury–Sherborne excursions. Yet another Class 5 to return to BR rails after a long absence was Carnforth's No. 44871 which made a return trip to Thornaby for tyre turning. Other notable first time steamings included *THE GREAT MARQUESS*, *BAHAMAS* and at the other end of the spectrum the diminutive Middleton Railway's Sentinel. It will be a total surprise if ever the latter sees main line service although it was noted on the North York Moors on the weekend of October 8th/9th working a three coach passenger train downhill from Goathland down to Grosmont! Since there are so many preserved Bulleid Pacifics it is not surprising that they get no more than a casual mention in a review of the year. *PORT LINE* became the first Merchant Navy to work on the Bluebell Railway and later in the year the inevitable happened; the side by side posing of 35027 and 35028 at Eastleigh. I wonder how long it will be before we can see three restored 'Merchants' together? The first of four Bulleid Pacifics destined for the Brighton Locomotive Works Preservation Group Nos. 34073 and 34046 moved to Brighton from Barry late in the year. In yet another transformation West Country No. 34010 *SIDMOUTH* lost its identity and became Battle of Britain No. 34109. The engine, which had been at Grosmont for many years awaiting restoration, was moved to private premises at Cargo Fleet, Teesside.

FLYING SCOTSMAN was in the news yet again when it set sail for an indefinite sojourn in Australia on 12th September.

Great Western Manor 4–6–0s hit the headlines too with No. 7822 hauling its first train out of Llangollen for the first time for many years. Meanwhile fully restored 7828 was on its way to the Gwili Railway via Barry looking very different indeed to the state it was in when it left the yard just seven years earlier. Indeed Barry itself was a very different place with all locos now sold; 8F 48173 was the 200th to leave, departing just 20 years after the first locomotive, Class 4F No.43924 was rescued.

PRINCESS ELIZABETH was among the exhibits at the Wolverton celebrations of the 150th anniversary of the London & Birmingham Railway, whilst sister locomotive *PRINCESS MARGARET* changed ownership, becoming the second locomotive in Brell Ewart's stable at Butterley. A return of the locomotive to main line running order is promised for the near future.

►Photographers are often branded as the 'pay nowt, see all' leeches of the preservation movement. This was handsomely proved not to be the case, if ever it was in doubt, when money was readily forthcoming to support the steaming of GW 2–8–0 No. 2857 for freight haulage on the SVR over the weekend 21st/22nd May. No. 2857, at the head of a superbly restored 16-wagon freight, is seen leaving Bewdley for Kidderminster late in the afternoon of 22nd May. Is it really over three years since this locomotive played out a similar GW 150 role on BR metals when it ran from Newport to Gloucester? The number of preserved GW 28XX 2–8–0s increased significantly during the year with another two leaving Dai Woodham's Barry scrapyard, one to the Wales Railway Centre and the other to the Birmingham Railway Museum. *Les Nixon*

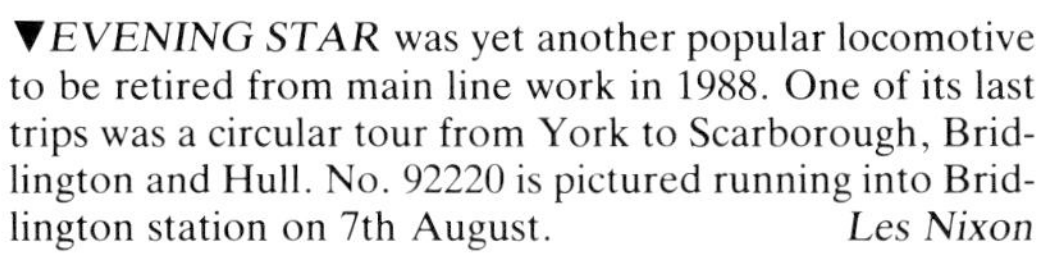

▼*EVENING STAR* was yet another popular locomotive to be retired from main line work in 1988. One of its last trips was a circular tour from York to Scarborough, Bridlington and Hull. No. 92220 is pictured running into Bridlington station on 7th August. *Les Nixon*

▼Yet another interesting and perhaps under-recorded locomotive transfer was the temporary loan of the charming North Yorkshire Moors Railway's Class J72 No. 69023 to the Yorkshire Dales Railway. The locomotive proved popular with crews and public alike although here it was caught by the camera in between duties being serviced at Embsay on 2nd October. *Brian Dobbs*

►The south bank of the River Mersey was the mecca for steam enthusiasts for May Day bank holiday weekend. An excellent transport extravaganza was organised by the Wirral Transport Society in support of the Lever Bros., Port Sunlight centenary celebrations. The company's 3 mile private railway system was host to GWR 2–6–2T No. 5572 and to Jinty No. 7298; the latter en route from Llangollen to the East Lancashire Railway at Bury. The pair worked five Mark 1 coaches in a push-pull operation from the BR station at Port Sunlight. In the heart of the works, where a reversal was necessary, No. 5572 became the lead engine for the run to the terminus. Other attractions included vintage bus services to the Port Sunlight 'model' village and a Hooton to Rock Ferry rail shuttle service operated by the maroon-liveried preserved Class 502 EMU. *Les Nixon*

▼1988 was a year of wanderlust for former Great Western locomotives. Two strangers found their way to the KWVR; Tyseley based pannier tank No. 7752 was the first visitor in the spring, while large-wheeled Prairie tank No. 6106 became the first locomotive of its class to work on the branch in late autumn. Even allowing for partisan attitudes the locomotive was singularly unpopular with locomotive crews; it certainly had more than its fair share of mechanical problems. No. 6106 was scheduled to be the only steam locomotive in service during the preserved diesel weekend of 5th/6th November but in the event it was withdrawn because of brake problems. In the snow clad landscape of the upper Worth Valley between Haworth and Oxenhope No. 6106 takes an afternoon train up the branch on 20th November. *Gavin Morrison*

▲The Gwili Railway was another Welsh system bidding for a place in the news during the year. In addition to acquiring the services of Manor No. 7828 *ODNEY MANOR* during the summer it was also host to pannier No. 7752. The sturdy tank is seen with four coaches climbing away from Cwmdwyfran with the 13.00 Bronwydd Arms to Llwyfan Cerrig on 6th April. *Hugh Ballantyne*

►Former GW 0–6–0PT No. 7752 again!! This much travelled loco was to be found in a number if countrywide locations during the year. In March it was at work on The KWVR, as noted above in high summer it was puffing away on the Gwili Railway in South Wales while in the autumn it was in steam back at Tyseley for the London & Birmingham 150th celebrations. As if this was not enough in between times on the weekend of 19th June it was guest of honour at Toddington where it is seen preparing to leave with the 15.30 departure to Winchcombe.
John B Gosling

◄*DEFIANT* became the fourth Castle to be returned to full working order, joining the ranks of exiled *PENDENNIS CASTLE; EARL BATHURST* and *CLUN CASTLE*. It made its first public run for 25 years on 11th June when it turned in a faultless performance with the Saltley–Didcot leg of the 'Red Dragon' excursion. The train is seen here passing the delightful Great Western setting at Dorrington, south of Shrewsbury.
Geoff Bannister

▲The LSW 150th celebrations on the western section of the Southern Region were centred on Salisbury and in particular on the operation of steam hauled specials to Andover, Romsey and Yeovil. Many enthusiasts were greatly disappointed by the news that King Arthur *SIR LAMIEL* would not be available, the more so when they discovered that the nominated substitute was 8F No. 48151 which (with no disrespect to this fine engine) was a type which was totally alien to the line. Nonetheless *CITY OF WELLS* was there to keep the Southern flag flying, which it did in fine style with some superb main line runs in addition to hauling some demonstration freight trains through Salisbury station. On 24th July it was photographed in full cry at Barford St Martin with a Salisbury–Yeovil special. *John Checkley*

►A typical latter-day Southern train, former USA Keighley based 0–6–0T No. 30072 and two bogie SR brake vans provided steam train rides during the Woking 150th weekend on 29th May. Other preserved steam locomotives at the event included No. 850 *LORD NELSON*, Class T9 No. 120, Class M7s Nos. 245/30053, No. 34092 *CITY OF WELLS* and Merchant Navy No. 35027 *PORT LINE*.
Chris Wilson

▲Preserved steam even found its way down to the sunny south coast of Bournemouth when Class 5 No. 5305 *ALDERMAN A. E. DRAPER* was brought down for the Open Day. The locomotive was moved in light steam from Marylebone on 26th March with Crompton No. 33113 providing the horses. The cavalcade is seen passing Eastleigh and Class 73 No. 73101 *BRIGHTON EVENING ARGUS* with a Bournemouth–Waterloo service.

Chris Wilson

▼In preparation for its use the following week on the Winchfield 150th Andover–Romsey workings, Class 4MT No. 80080 worked a Salisbury–Sherborne test and press train on Monday, 19th September. It then ran ecs to Yeovil to turn, but here the tank stands at Salisbury at 21.15 after working the return trip. With the departure of Gerald Daniels, the Salisbury Area Manager, to pastures new it is probable that 1988 will prove to be the last year for the operation of preserved steam on this section of the old London and South Western main line.

Geoff Gillham

STEAM LOCOMOTIVES PRESERVED FROM BARRY:

No.	*Moved to*	*Date*	*No.*	*Moved to*	*Date*
2861	Wales Railway Centre	22/02/88	34073	Brighton Railway Museum	21/02/88
2873	Birmingham Railway Museum	30/03/88	35009	Brighton Railway Museum	/ /88
4115	Wales Railway Centre	02/03/88	44901	Wales Railway Centre	29/02/88
5227	Wales Railway Centre	15/02/88	48173	Avon Valley Railway	14/09/88
5539	Wales Railway Centre	01/03/88	48518	Wales Railway Centre	19/02/88
6686	Wales Railway Centre	18/02/88	80072	Swindon Heritage Centre	/07/88
7927	Wales Railway Centre	23/02/88	80150	Wales Railway Centre	17/02/88
34046	Brighton Railway Museum	/08/88	92245	Wales Railway Centre	16/02/88

◀Few former LNWR locomotives survive and the opportunity was taken to rescue the National Railway Museum Super D 0–8–0 from open air display at the Blists Hill Museum at Telford to join veteran 2–2–2 *CORNWALL*. Although No. 9395 looked spick and span, restoration was purely cosmetic and there are no plans at present to return it to full working order. Alongside is another LMS exhibit Jubilee No. 5593 *KOLHAPUR*.
Hugh Ballantyne

◄Although the East Coast main line was the centre of attention in 1988 the West Coast route had its counter-attraction in the shape of the London & Birmingham 150th celebrations. Tyseley was host to a number of visiting steam locomotives for a celebration weekend in mid-September. Somewhat inappropriately, in this scene former GWR rather than 'Premier' line locomotives take pride of place around the turntable at Tyseley. Featured from left to right are Castle No. 7029 *CLUN CASTLE*, 0-6-0PT No. 7752, Didcot-based Castle No. 5080 *DEFIANT*, 0-6-0PT No. 7760 and tow industrial saddle tanks. Centre stage is the NRM replica *ROCKET* which was being manoeuvred into its display position. *Hugh Ballantyne*

PHOENIX STEAM

►*BAHAMAS* - the unique double chimneyed Jubilee has been out of action for almost 15 years; restoration to main line order has at times seemed painfully slow but the Dinting restorers can be justly proud of the end product seen here on press launch day, 22nd September. Bereft of a few cosmetic details, such as some of the lining out and BR emblems, it seemed a lion in a very small cage as it steamed along the short branch. A main line ticket is expected early in 1989 and the locomotive is promised for next season's North Wales excursions. *Les Nixon*

▼Yet another Bulleid Pacific to be returned to full working order was Merchant Navy No. 35027 *PORT LINE* although it is only the second locomotive of its class to reach this status. The locomotive became the first Merchant Navy to steam over the Bluebell line and it is pictured here climbing towards Horsted Keynes on 18th June, appropriately with matching Bulleid malachite green liveried stock in tow. *David Brown*

▲ In their heyday the 'Westerns' enjoyed a long association with West of England services. Ironically, although no fewer than seven examples escaped the cutter's torch, the nearest one has got to their old Cornish haunts since withdrawal in 1976 was the appearance of D1023 *WESTERN FUSILIER* on the Dart Valley Railway in 1987. 1988 was the year of the return of a diesel hydraulic to the Duchy when D1048 was moved from exile at the Steamport Railway Museum to the Bodmin & Wenford Railway. *WESTERN LADY* commenced her journey from Southport on 11th July and en route it was commandeered by Laira TMD for their open day. Here she looks spick and span and a centre of attention at the depot on 17th July. *Stephen Widdowson*

▼Another 'Western' diesel hydraulic to hit the headlines early in the year was East Lancashire Railway's No. D1041 *WESTERN PRINCE* which was fully refurbished by BREL, Crewe in January. Resplendent in original maroon livery the locomotive stands in the works yard on 12th February. *Colin J Marsden*

▲Inevitably the death throes of Class 25s in BR service crystallised the thoughts of many preservationists. Perhaps the 'Rats' were not the most loved of the first generation diesels but they are ideal machines for economical, short distance, low speed haulage of medium weight trains – perfect for our preserved lines. No. 25191 was obtained by the NYMR in 1987 and in the spring of 1988 it was pressed into revenue-earning service. Here it is still in its rather grubby standard BR blue livery as it takes six coaches down the bank towards Grosmont at Darnholm on 23rd April.
Gavin Morrison

►One of the six Class 25s to be preserved during the year was No. 25057, formerly D 5207, which is pictured at the Buckinghamshire Railway Centre on 6th August, shortly after its move from Vic Berry's yard at Leicester.
A.O.Wynn

DIESEL LOCOMOTIVES PRESERVED

Nos. Carried		*Location*
D 99	45135	Peak Rail, Matlock
D 200	40106	National Railway Museum
D 212	40012	Midland Railway Centre
D 213	40013	South Yorkshire Railway
D 318	40118	Birmingham Railway Museum
D 335	40135	East Lancashire Railway
D 1842	47192	Crewe Heritage Centre
D 2059	03059	Isle of Wight Steam Railway
D 2063	03063	Colne Valley Railway
D 2078	03078	Stephenson Railway Museum
D 2334		South Yorkshire Railway
D 2337		South Yorkshire Railway
D 3452		Bodmin and Wenford Railway
D 3476		South Yorkshire Railway
D 4092		South Yorkshire Railway
D 5185	25035	Northampton Steam Railway
D 5207	25057	Buckinghamshire Railway Centre
D 5222	25072	Swindon & Cricklade Railway
D 5233	25083	Crewe Heritage Centre
D 7612	25262*	Privately preserved
D 7659	25309*	East Lancashire Railway

* Also carried 25901 and 25909 respectively.

▲The South Yorkshire Railway can lay claim to being the most travelled preservation society in the country. The group made what is hoped to be their final move in 1988 and are now in residence at Meadowhall, Sheffield, their fourth site in just about as many years. Initially they occupied the goods yard at Penistone, then part of the Newton Chambers complex at Chapeltown, then a less than ideal spot in 'downtown' Attercliffe. The imminent development of this area as part of a site for the 1991 Student Games prompted Sheffield Council to reverse their original decision to support the development of the line at this location. The Council paid for the not inconsiderable expense of relocation down the road to a spot just east of Wincobank Junction on the Sheffield–Rotherham main line which is close to the M1 and the new Meadowhall super leisure complex. More importantly, track is still in situ on the nearby remnant of the former GCR Sheffield Victoria–Ecclesfield line so there is a real prospect that train services will be resumed once again in the not too distant future. At present the Society has acquired a unique collection of former BR diesel shunters including representatives of Classes 01, 02, 03, 04, 06, 07, 08 and 10. In this view taken on 17th December the spacious yard at Meadowhall can be seen with Class 01 No. D2953 in the foreground and in the distance the connection to the Ecclesfield line. *Les Nixon*

◄Two preserved electric locomotives doing the rounds of open days during the year were the former Woodhead Class EM2 Co–Co No. 27000 *ELECTRA* and Class 71 No. E5001. No. 27000, now restored to unlined green livery following its retirement from service in Netherlands Railways, is pictured here at the Bescot open day on 9th October. It was also present at Winchfield 150th and at Waterloo on Network South East day, 1st October. E5001 equally resplendent in its 1960s green livery was also photographed at Waterloo on the same day. *Stephen Widdowson*

▲Tank engines in main line service continued to be something of a novelty on BR, a fact which made the appearance of Butterley's standard Class 4MT 2–6–4T on the Nottingham–Derby–Matlock excursions on 22nd May even more attractive than usual. Here No. 80080 makes a smokey exit from Nottingham with the morning outward bound trip to Matlock. *Hugh Ballantyne*

▼Particular credit must go to the dedicated band of volunteers of the Middleton Railway who undertook a superb restoration job on the former LNER Class Y1 Sentinel, formerly BR No. 68153. Restored to BR unlined black livery and carrying Departmental Number 54 it was even seen in action on the North Yorkshire Moors Railway during the weekend of 8th/9th October when it was noted in sole charge of a three coach train – downhill from Goathland to Grosmont! However, in this delightful night scene it is back home at the Middleton Railway, Leeds on 27th November. *Doug Birmingham*

▲The return of Manor No. 7822 *FOXCOTE MANOR* to revenue earning service was a notable milestone in the short history of the Llangollen Railway. Congratulations were certainly in order if the appearance of this train, the 1300 Llangollen–Berwyn on 10th April, was anything to go by. The superbly restored BR green livery of the Manor was perfectly complemented by the chocolate and cream stock. *Brian Dobbs*

▼*MALLARD's* farewell to main line duty was on 27th August when it hauled a 13 coach train southbound over the Settle and Carlisle line. Much to the surprise of the many enthusiasts who had congregated by the lineside at Birkett, the location of this photograph, the train approached at a sedate walking pace and stopped just short of the tunnel. Amazingly the A4 had run out of steam; a result of a bout of priming which converted soot on the spark arrester to an impermeable barrier. This drastically reduced the draught through the boiler; but emergency work at Garsdale soon restored the A4's reputation of being one of the best steaming locomotives ever to run on BR. *Les Nixon*

▲Sanders on, feather of steam at the safety valves and a fine plume of smoke add up to a fitting tribute to the final BR outing of one of our best loved main line steamers, *CITY OF WELLS*. Expiry of the boiler certificate will enforce main line retirement, at least for 1989. No. 34092 was photographed near Newbiggin recovering from a Culgaith signal check with a southbound Settle & Carlisle line excursion on 22nd October 1988. *Les Nixon*

▼In complete contrast, an example of the hare and the tortoise perhaps, is 8F No. 48151 leaving Appleby on 12 November. In 1988 this Stanier Black 8 became the first member of its class in preserved condition to take a passenger train over the Settle and Carlisle line. It performed impeccably on all of its trips and has established itself as a firm favourite among enthusiasts. About an hour before this picture was taken a serious fire on board *ETHEL* 2 had just been extinguished. Delighted enthusiasts hoped that the *ETHEL* would be scrapped but it has since been repaired and soldiers on to upset steam bashers and to spoil yet more tape recordings and photographs. *Les Nixon*

▲As soon as the Foster Yeoman Class 59s entered traffic, enthusiasts began rubbing crystal balls to pedict the first date on which one would be used for the benefit of haulage bashers. Union disputes have precluded their use on passenger trains on BR track but No. 59001 *YEOMAN ENDEAVOUR* was able to show its paces during the SVR diesel weekend of 20th April. Enthusiasts were spoilt for choice; Class 37/4 No. 37427, Class 31/4 No. 31413 and Class 20 No. 20170 were BR representatives – however, our bet is that visitors weren't exactly queueing to travel on Sprinter No. 156 404! Insurance problems regarding the running of BR diesels on private railways meant problems later in 1988 for similar occurrences. Here the stranger is seen leaving Bewdley Tunnel with the 14.41 Kidderminster–Bridgnorth on the 7th May. *Melville Holley*

▼London Underground's 1986 prototype tube stock went into public service during 1988. The rear of a six-car train is seen at Willesden Green on 19th July formed of two red and four green cars on a Wembley Park–Charing Cross working. *Kevin Lane*

LONDON UNDERGROUND

It is perhaps inevitable that the year should be dominated by the events following the King's Cross fire disaster of the previous November. The subsequent investigation, culminating in the Fennell Report published on November 10th, made many recommendations. These included a replacement programme of escalators, the substitution of wood for metal in certain escalator sections and the introduction of heat detectors and sprinklers beneath the escalators; that there should be a general improvement of cleanliness all round; a closer co-operation with the emergency services, and better staff training in the event of a similar situation. The publication of the report led to the immediate resignation of London Underground's Chairman Dr Tony Ridley, to be replaced by Sir Neil Shields.

Restoration work at King's Cross, the busiest station on the system, began early in the year, while in November, and with the prospect of a Channel Tunnel terminal being sited nearby, plans for an enlarged new station were announced.

Increased passenger safety has also been a feature of the Underground in 1988. A £3.5 m scheme of security measures was launched in April to curb the disturbing increase in crime on the system, including a number of help point booths, manned during the peak periods and in the evenings, the equipping of staff with two-way radios, more close-circuit televisions at stations and a general improvement in such areas as lighting.

Radical changes in the organisational structure of the Underground was announced in November. It was recognised that each line had its own separate identity, and it was decided to run each as a business unit with its own general manager. Interestingly, the East London Line is treated as a separate unit as is the grouped Hammersmith & City and Circle Lines. Each general manager will report to the passenger services director. The principle of the new structure is to give every member of staff an individual to report to rather than various shift supervisors. These units will form a core, around which the company will be structured. Major policy will be the responsibility of a new executive board, chaired by Denis Tunnicliffe.

Station and line improvements continued throughout the year. Projects completed included new ticket halls at Tower Hill and Liverpool Street, while new plans announced included a massive £720 m Central Line modernisation, which will also provide for new trains and signalling, investments into the Northern Line, and more general improvements such as more dot matrix destination indicators, the installation of public telephones on platforms (the first was put into use at Victoria on the District Line in November) and a major lifts and escalators replacement programme.

On the rolling stock front, the prototype trains for the Central Line went into revenue service on the Jubilee Line in May, while later in the same month saw the retirement of the red 1938 stock from the Northern. Graffiti vandalism has worsened, two youths died for their 'art' during the year. To combat the problem, a graffiti-proof paint was applied to an 'A' stock train on the East London Line. Finally, October 2nd saw another eye-catching railtour organised by the Underground, in this case two Gatwick sets between a pair of battery locomotives. Long may such spectacles continue; what price a preserved pannier around the Inner Circle, I wonder?!

▲The 1986 Prototype Tube Stock made its public debut on May 4th on the Jubilee Line, initially formed of two cars from each of the three four-car trains delivered in 1986/7. Each train carries a different livery: Red for train 'A', built by Metro-Cammell with traction equipment by GEC Transportation Projects, blue for train 'B', built by BREL at Derby with Brush traction equipment, while train 'C' is green, also built by Metro-Cammell (and using the same body-shell as train 'A') but with traction equipment by Brown-Boveri, Zurich. Many new features have been incorporated into the design, both in technical and passenger comfort terms, and the final production trains will form part of the £500 million Central Line modernisation programme, due in the 1990s. The green four-car set leads two cars from the red train into the platform at Wembley Park on July 19th, to take up service to Charing Cross.
Kevin Lane

◀Shortly after the entry into service of the Underground's newest train, we said goodbye to its oldest. In 1986 five trains of 1938 stock were returned to service on the Northern Line in order to meet an increase in passengers, their reprieve lasting nearly two years. The last train ran on May 19th, while a seven-car unit was seen at the former GNR terminus at High Barnet on a Morden-bound train on April 27th. It is not quite the end yet, for some trains will be taking the place of pre-1938 stock on the Isle of Wight from early 1989.
Mike Haddon

▼To counter the increasing threat of graffiti vandalism, a four-car train of A60 stock has been coated with specially protective paint, including a combing primer, finish and lacquer which will greatly aid the removal of graffiti. The repainted train will bring a splash of colour to the East London Line, with its red ends, blue doors and grey roof, together with a new-style interior. Sponsored 75% by the London Docklands Development Corporation, the train was launched on November 16th. The unit, Driving Motor car 5066 leading, waits at New Cross Gate on December 28th on a Whitechapel working.
Brian Morrison

►A close-up of the Underground and London Docklands logos, applied to the anti-graffiti train on the New Cross–Whitechapel East London Line. *Brian Morrison*

▼A £20 m rebuilding of Angel station on the Northern Line was given government approval on August 17th. The work will involve diverting the northbound track (on the right-hand side of the picture) into a new tunnel, incorporating a platform. With the southbound track left where it is, filling in of the old northbound trackbed will give a much wider platform. A new concourse, escalators and booking hall is also a feature of the plan. Only two other stations retain island tunnel platforms in this form, at Clapham Common and Clapham North, also on the Northern Line. The picture shows a Morden-bound train of 1972 stock leaving Angel on November 5th. *Kevin Lane*

An upsurge in traffic on the Bakerloo Line saw the return of off-peak services through to Harrow & Wealdstone from May and an increase in the number of trains on the Stonebridge Park–Queens Park–Elephant & Castle section from October. A seven-car train of 1972 Mark 2 stock reverses at Harrow, passing the former No 2 signal box on December 20th. *Kevin Lane*

LIGHT RAIL TRANSIT

Many steps towards the introduction of Light Rail Transit into UK cities took place during 1988, but only one building contract was commenced, this being the Bank extension of the Docklands Light Railway.

At the start of the year, parliamentary powers were still being sought for three Greater Manchester bills, together with one each for South Yorkshire PTE, Advanced Transport for Avon Ltd and Docklands Light Railway Limited. However, to the great delight of the supporters of LRT, two of the Manchester bills and the South Yorkshire bill received Royal Assent during the year and, with many and varied schemes being investigated, the future looks quite bright.

Due to this increasing interest in LRT in the UK, it has been decided to comment on developments during 1988, both to existing and proposed systems, in system/scheme order. Hopefully this will help the reader to see what is happening and where.

TYNE & WEAR METRO

Although very much involved in the effects of bus deregulation this system continued to operate efficiently during the year. However, some administrative disruption was caused when three senior executives were suspended due to their involvement in a plan to purchase the Metro system. On a more positive note, the PTE deposited a bill to Parliament in November seeking powers to extend the system by 4 km from Bankfoot to Newcastle International Airport. Financing will come from the Airport Authority, the PTA, private investors and European Regional Development Grant. On November 6th, entry barriers at all suburban stations were abolished and, at the same time, more revenue control inspectors were engaged.

DOCKLANDS LIGHT RAILWAY

Passenger journeys on the initial line are now in the region of 20,000 per day. The private bill for the Beckton extension has been opposed in the House of Commons on the grounds that the wrong alignment has been selected, and consequently this has caused a delay in its progress. Everybody concerned is of the opinion that the line should be constructed.

Work commenced on March 14th, on the Bank Extension, which will cost in the region of £150 m of which approximately £68 m will be provided by Olympia & York (Canary Wharf) Ltd, with the remainder coming from government grants. The Beckton Extension will be financed by London Docklands Development Corporation through land sales.

Towards the end of the year the London Boroughs of Greenwich and Lewisham joined the LDDC and London Regional Transport on a co-ordinating group set up to investigate the planning, engineering and financial aspects of an extension beneath the River Thames to the named boroughs.

On a more general note it is sad to see how Docklands contrasts with Paris's new commercial centre at La Défense. In Docklands, steps are only now being taken to extend the DLR, raise its capacity (and improve the area's woefully inadequate road systems). The French government first built the limited-stop, 90 mph Réseau Express Regional (RER) and good roads to link the development to the rest of Paris and Charles de Gaulle airport; only then did it free land onto the market.

GREATER MANCHESTER PTE

On the 18th January 1988, the then Minister of State for Transport David Mitchell, announced to the House of Commons, that the government endorsed the Greater Manchester PTE's LRT proposals and that a section 56 grant of up to 50% of the cost could be forthcoming if the scheme attracted private sector backing.

He said that the government required a private sector build, operate and maintain agreement on behalf of the PTE. After this announcement detail design was commenced with special emphasis on low-floor vehicle design and city centre station design with disabled accessibility.

◄A mock-up of the proposed GMPTE 'Metrolink' city centre station design was exhibited at Birchfields Road in Manchester. The stations will have low platforms with a raised section at one end to allow pram/wheelchair access. *David Holt*

►An artists impression of a Greater Manchester LRV running through St. Peter's Square in the centre of Manchester at street level. This will form part of the first route from Altrincham to Bury. A second LRV can be seen standing at the proposed station. *GMPTE*

Royal Assent was duly granted on the 9th February to the first two bills. To implement the scheme effectively it was considered important to involve the public in the design. An LRT Project Consultative Committee was therefore set up under the Greater Manchester Transportation Consultative Committee.

In May 1988, newspaper advertisements appeared inviting suitably experienced companies to register their interest on a select list of tenders to design, build, operate and maintain the first phase of the LRT system. By September eight consortia were named as follows:- CIE Consult, Fairclough/Transmark, GMA Group, Hawker Siddeley/Norwest Holst and Rosehaugh, Trafalgar House/BREL, TNT-Man RT Systems/Simon Carver, Wimpey Abb Traction A.B.

A new company was set up during the middle of the year, by the PTE, to operate the concession. Its managing director (designate) was named as Mr D. S. Hellewell. At about this same time (22nd June) it was announced that the name "Metrolink" had been selected for the system.

During July, a mock up LRV and the proposed profiled platform were put on view for the press and public. This exercise was repeated for the public in November.

In the same month, the PTE submitted its fourth bill to Parliament, this time for powers to extend the system to Trafford Park, Oldham, Rochdale and Chorlton.

ADVANCED TRANSPORT FOR AVON LTD

The bill submitted to the House of Lords in November 1987, asking for Powers for a private company to develop a LRT system in Bristol/Avon area reached the Commons and received its first reading on 7th June. The proceedings were halted by an objection by the Bristol South MP (Ms. Primarolo) on the grounds that all implications in the bill had not been correctly worked through. This objection has forced a second reading, debate on which will take place in 1989. Further objections have also to be overcome from Bristol City Council, British Rail and a private company. However, even allowing for the opposition, a £40 m contract which is dependent on the passing of the bill, has been entered into with Hawker Siddeley Rail Projects and Balfour Beatty to design, equip and construct the first phase line.

The second bill for extension of the scheme to serve Bristol city centre at street level and extending outwards to Yate, did not materialise as expected in November. The company apparently agreed with the Avon County Council and Bristol City Council to delay the bill to allow more discussion regarding the city centre alignment.

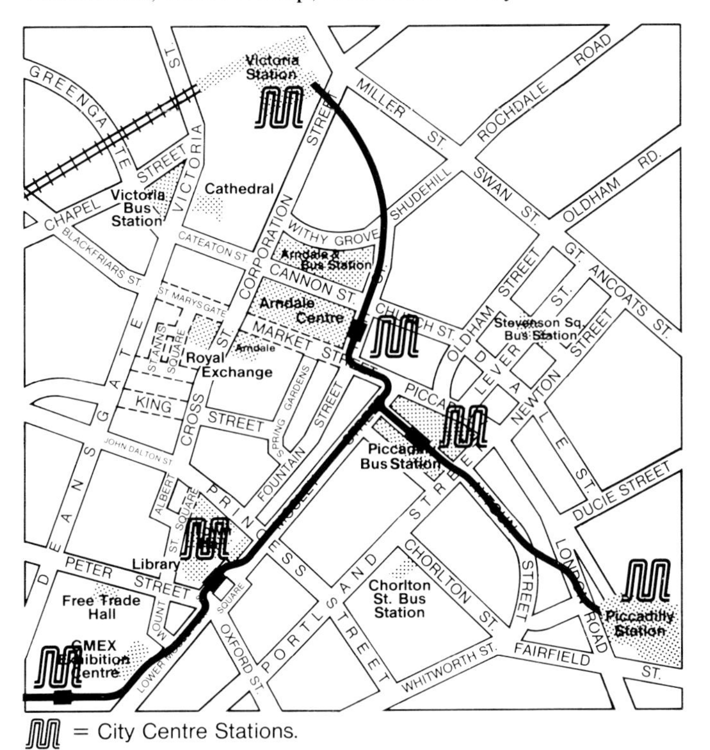

The map shows the route of 'Metrolink' through Central Manchester.
GMPTE

WEST MIDLANDS PTE

At £800 m, the whole of the Midland Metro plans must rank as the biggest local authority project for many years. Considerable private sector backing is, however, reported for this scheme, with Trafalgar House and Tarmac Construction expressing interest. The PTA has set up a company named Midlands Metro Ltd to allow private and public participation.

On 18th February 1988 the WMPTA announced that a bill would be submitted to Parliament in November and the first phase would be from Birmingham to Wolverhampton mainly on former rail alignment but with street running in the latter.

WEST YORKSHIRE PTE

Consultants Steer, Davies & Gleave were appointed during the year to examine the feasibility of a £38 m surface LRT scheme for East Leeds. The outcome of this work was the submission of a bill to Parliament in November. However, a few days after the submission Leeds City Council made known its opposition to the scheme and the bill was withdrawn so that further studies could take place. Apparently Leeds City Council would like automated guideway systems investigated as well.

SOUTH YORKSHIRE PTE

On 24th February 1988, the South Yorkshire Passenger Transport Authority announced an investigation of a Supertram line in Sheffield's Lower Don Valley. This investigation had to take into account the possibility of an extension of the line into Rotherham at a later date, and followed Sheffield City Council's support of the first bill for Supertram between Hillsborough and Mosborough. Following this announcement the PTE appointed the MVA Consultancy to lead a joint study team, which had to adhere to a very tight timetable to meet the target of submitting a bill to Parliament in November. This study culminated in the choice of a combined road/rail alignment via Cricket Inn Road/Woodbourn Road, and eventually running alongside the ex GCR line to Meadowhall. The conclusions were endorsed by the PTA on the 22nd July. Meanwhile the Line 1 bill resumed its Commons Hearing on 13th April when the city council presented a petition against alteration of the bill. Objections were heard by the select committee from National Car Parks and two local residents which were duly overuled. This allowed the bill to be transferred to The Lords where an amazing 55 petitions were deposited against the bill mainly from residents and traders who claimed the proposals would directly affect them or their property. Of these petitioners a small number appeared in person in committee together with representatives from the Sheffield Chamber of Trade between 6th and 15th July. The committee chairman announced that after considering the petitions the committee were of the opinion that the bill should proceed. This it did and finally received Royal Assent on 27th October.

In September, newspaper advertisements appeared inviting interested organisations to register their interest in future tendering by 31st October. By November, the local press stated that over 100 firms in Britain and Europe had registered.

◄Artist's impression of a Supertram under the M1 Tinsley Viaduct. This section of the SYPTE proposed line 2 would run along the former Great Central Railway route from Tinsley South Junction to Wath and Barnsley, latterly cut back to Smithywood Colliery. To the right will be the new Meadowhall shopping and leisure development. *SYPTE*

▼Route of the proposed SYPTE Supertram line 2. The route passes the new athletics stadium being constructed for the World Student Games in 1991 and terminates at the new Meadowhall bus/rail/tram interchange. Future extensions are planned to Rotherham and to the Tinsley Airport ('Stolport'). *SYPTE*

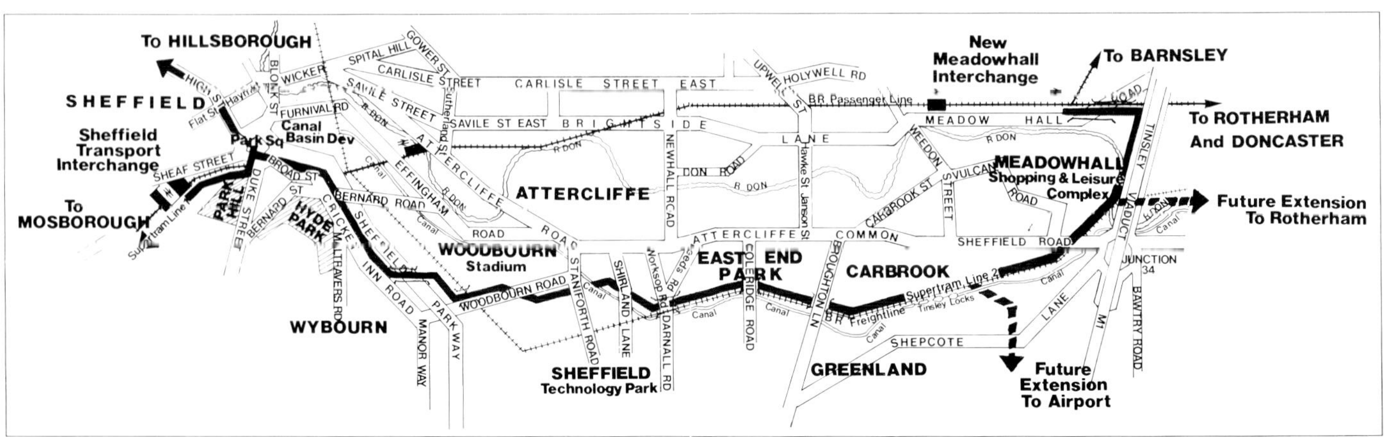

SOUTHAMPTON

After feasibility studies looking at both surface LRT and elevated 'peoplemover' systems were completed, a bill was deposited in November for the latter. However, due to considerable opposition the proposed scheme has been considerably shortened and doubts are being expressed regarding the whole project.

OTHER UK SCHEMES

Many other cities/counties have made known their interest during 1988 and these are listed below. However, as all these proposals are at an early stage no attempt is made to comment individually. The schemes are Aberdeen, Cardiff, Cambridge, Croydon, Cleveland, Mid Devon, Edinburgh, Glasgow, Hampshire, Liverpool, Nottingham, Norwich and Stoke on Trent.

Tourist tramway schemes are also envisaged for Gloucester and Newcastle Quayside.

▲Karlsruhe's light rail vehices will soon be running under DB 15 kV ac overhead as part of a regional scheme to integrate tram and train services. These 'Stadtbahn' cars already run over a DB diesel freight line which has been electrified at 750 V dc. This set was photographed at Ittersbach on the 'Albtalbahn' which runs from Ittersbach, across Karlsruhe to Neureut.
John Priestley

GENERAL

On more general points, it was announced in May that Mr Martin Shrubsole had been appointed to a new post of project director light rapid transit BR Provincial, reporting directly to Sidney Newey. The position is responsible for developing and implementing the BR strategy for its involvement with all prospective LRT systems outside London. BR is aware of the possible benefits to cities of well-planned LRT systems.

The report of the joint committee on private bill procedure criticised the way LRT schemes have to be presented. This came as a direct complaint from South Yorkshire PTE who expressed concern over the undue length and expense incurred and for obtaining too narrow a consultation procedure. The committee stated it agreed with the SYPTE that the Tramways Act 1870 needs considerable updating and revision to meet modern requirements and that there is no more need in principle for Parliament to be concerned with trams than it is with lorries.

EUROPE

On mainland Europe, 1988 brought a period of expansion of systems rather than new ones. Extensions were under way in the cities of Amsterdam, Den Haag, Köln, Düsseldorf, Essen, Bonn, Krefeld, Freiberg, Stuttgart, Würzburg, Nantes, Valencia, Genova, Goteborg and Wien. However, the closure of the Trondheim system in June must sadly be recorded.

It was announced during the year that planners are looking at the possibility of linking the Rotterdam and Den Haag tramway systems by the conversion of the N.S. 'Hofpleinlijn' to Light Rail operation.

Grenoble car 2020 was on loan to Rotterdam tramways for a month in July/August, and München was reported to have ordered three prototype low floor vehicles. These are the first new orders for tramway vehicles in München for a few years. Hopefully the future of this fine system will now be secure.

Finally, an interesting agreement was signed in November to allow inter-running of German Federal Railway's local services with the Karlsruhe light rail network, using dual voltage trams with a 15kV power supply capability in addition to the normal low voltage dc system.

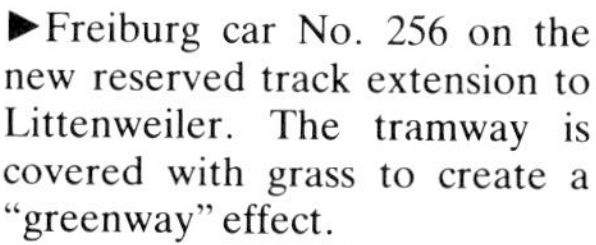

►Freiburg car No. 256 on the new reserved track extension to Littenweiler. The tramway is covered with grass to create a "greenway" effect.
F.A. Andrews

EUROPEAN SCENE

AUSTRIA

After the 150th anniversary celebrations in 1987 ÖBB started 1988 by putting itself under the microscope and came up with a programme of line closures with the new timetable in May. However, it was not all doom and gloom as improvements were also part of the package. In a departure from normal continental practice ÖBB started bringing in local improvements as early as possible instead of adhering to timetable change dates. New marketing initiatives also followed and many of the improved services have been runaway successes. However, this is not altogether surprising for on some branch lines patterns of service had not altered much since early post-war days.

Complete closures:

11a Markt St.Ägyd–Kernhof
11b Mariazell–Gusswerk
12a Kienberg Gaming–Lunz am See
52 Bierbaum–Neudau
52a Oberwart–Oberschützen
61 Vordernberg Markt–Krumpenthal
93a Gaweinstal–Passdorf Lokalbahn
93c Enzersdorf bei Staaz–Poysdorf
93d Stammersdorf–Obersdorf, Sulz Nexing–Zistersdorf Stadt, Zistersdorf–Dobermannsdorf
? Laa a. d. Thaya–Wildendünbach.

Passenger services withdrawn:

52g Deutschkreuz–Oberpullendorf
61 Eisenerz–Krumpenthal
93a Gross Schweinbarth–Gaweinstal, Paasdorf Lokalbahn–Mistelbahn Lokalbahn
93d Pirawarth–Sulz-Nexing, Zistersdorf–Dobermannsdorf
94a Korneuberg–Mistelbach Lokalbahn
94c Sigmundsherberg–Laa a. d. Thaya Stadt.

As can be seen, the lines to the north of Wien were particularly hard hit. However, on the sections of lines 93a and 93d that remained open, improved services using the new one man-operated diesel railcars of Class 5047 were introduced and have been a great success, with trains having to be strengthened. Later in the year ÖBB introduced a package of improvements to services in Burgenland from 1st September whilst from 14th December electrified services were introduced between Spittal–Millstättersee and Lienz. Other improvements were also announced for introduction early in 1989. Another line electrified in 1988 was the short section from Vordernberg to Vordernberg Markt.

EC 'Lehar'. This new service between Wien and Budapest is the only EC train into the Eastern Bloc. It is worked by ÖBB Class 1146 dual-voltage locos. The service has been very popular and at public holidays has run in triplicate, such has been the demand. To balance the use of ÖBB locos in Hungary, MAV M62 diesels now have duties to Graz working through from Szombathely and even have a fill-in turn to Gleisdorf.

Neue Bahn is the title given to ÖBB's scheme for long-term modernisation plans to take the system into the next century. Amongst projects being looked at are the closure of Wien Westbhf and diversion of trains to an enlarged Südbahnhof which will become Wien Central. Other plans include a Semmering Basis Tunnel and an avoiding line around Innsbruck. A new high speed line may be constructed in the south of the country whilst other lines will be upgraded for higher speeds. During the year ÖBB tested the Italian 'Pendolino' and the Spanish 'Talgo Pendular' tilting trains in its search for higher speeds. Later orders were placed for three 6-car Italian trains.

Motive Power. No great changes in the year. Delivery of further Class 1063 electric shunting locos allowed older types to be withdrawn whilst the success of the Class 5047 DMUs meant a little lease of life for older units which could not be spared. It is now expected that new driving trailers will have to be built for the 5047s.

Private Lines. The main event of 1988 was the electrification of the GySEV line from Sopron to Ebenfurth.

Steam Scene. A quiet year compared to 1987. However, ÖBB continued running steam excursions in 1988 and offered a varied programme which was deemed successful. On the preservation front some more locos came off plinths and changed owners etc. whilst ÖGEG found it slow progress restoring its Romanian 2–8–4. The main event of the year must be the opening of a new museum line operation when the Taurachbahn started running between Mauterndorf and St. Andrä using 699.01. 52.3314 and 93.1422 left Austria for new owners in West Germany.

BELGIUM

Belgian Railways in 1988 were still in a state of limbo but showed some signs of recovery. Electrification of the Namur–Dinant line still has to be completed but Jurbise–Ath–Geraardsbergen did get finished in time for the new timetable. This allowed Enghien–Braine le Comte to be closed completely. Some other lines lost their passenger services during the year notably Ronse–Leuze, Athus–Autelbas, Dinant–Givet whilst local trains were withdrawn between Welkenraedt and Aachen. On the credit side the summer timetable saw 12 stations reopened and some extra trains being put on, especially late evening.

Motive Power. The continuing rationalisation of freight services allowed the withdrawal of all remaining examples of Class 59 and 60 whilst many Class 80 shunters were also laid up. Some withdrawn locos were sold to Italy. The last Class 43 DMUs also ceased use in passenger service although there are some in departmental use.

New deliveries saw the completion of the order for Class 21 electric locos and production of Class 900 series EMUs commenced. This class brought yet another unusual looking front end on to the Belgian scene. Also new were the 2-car postal units converted from Type 54 EMUs. These are known officially as Type 54P but carry a large 'POSTE 90' logo.

Finally, Belgium lost two international routes as Comines–Armentières and Quiévrain–Blanc Misseron freight lines were closed during the year. However, another line that has seen little use recently had passenger trains for the first time in many years when the SNCF ran their beach trains from Lille to Bray Dunes through to De Panne on Sundays in the summer.

DENMARK DSB

A rather quiet year with electrification slowly creeping out from København and services starting to Roskilde. This resulted in some diesels being made surplus to requirements and which have been sold to private lines. The first of the new IC3 DMUs was produced in time to be exhibited at the IVA in Hamburg. It is reported that the building of this set has nearly bankrupted the builder but an increase in the order to 50 sets will no doubt cushion the blow. The Great Belt project got underway and is scheduled for completion in 1993. This new tunnel/bridge connection will mean big changes in traffic flows with the possibility of much freight traffic being diverted this way between Denmark and West Germany.

FINLAND

Another railway that has had a hard look at itself resulting in a reorganisation with some sectorisation coming in and a lot of decision making put out to local levels. Locos and rolling stock started to appear in the new liveries and the IC services between Helsinki and Vaasa and Imatra were amongst the first to get the new look. Here too there were closures with some passenger services being withdrawn with the summer timetable allowing the withdrawal of all remaining DMUs.

FRANCE

SNCF

An otherwise successful year was marred by a series of tragic accidents. The Paris Gare de Lyon crash (27th June) received widespread publicity in the UK but there were also other bad crashes at Paris Gare de l'Est (6th August) and Ays and even a Grenoble–Paris TGV crashed on 23rd September. This last incident was not on the LGV route itself but was a Hixon-type accident when a large transformer en route from Italy got stuck on a level crossing.

On the positive side there were many improvements to train services. Electrified services that were introduced during the year included the VMI suburban link in Paris, Don Sainghin–Bethune, Moret–Nevers, Mont St. Martin–Athus and St. Pierre d'Albigny to Bourg St. Maurice. The last mentioned was completed in time for TGV Ski specials to operate during the winter.

TGV. TGVs were also in the news in other areas. The route of TGV Nord was announced and it did not include Amiens. This town was disgusted at not being on the route and there were many demonstrations demanding it be included. Compare that to the attitude in Kent! TGV Atlantique construction continued and the first section was energised. The first sets for the new line were also delivered and began trial running. It was fully expected that they would enter service on ordinary schedules early in 1989.

Several high speed test runs were made during the year aimed, no doubt at setting a high speed for the German ICE to beat – which it did. Finally, whilst still on the TGV theme a Lille–Nice TGV was introduced on Saturdays in the summer.

Besides building TGVs, Alsthom was also busy building the first of the new dual-voltage locos of Class 26000 – the 'Sybics' (Synchronous-Bicourant). The first locos were nominally allocated to Dijon but most were engaged on one sort of test or another during the year and the home depot saw little of them. They were expected to go into regular service towards the end of 1988. Another new type to be delivered was the Z 20500 double-deck EMU for use on the Paris area services from the Gare du Nord, in particular RER'D'.

Refurbishing of older types continued with CC 7100 back in favour at the expense of BB 9400s. Many DMUs were facelifted and some received new style front ends. Others were painted in regional liveries to reflect the subsidy paid by local authorities. The year also saw some old favourites disappearing. The last X 3800 'Picasso' type DMUs finished regular service at Bordeaux being replaced by new X 2200s based at Limoges. Many of these strange railcars have, however, been preserved. The CC 65000 diesel locos also finished operation as a result of spare locos being released by electrification extensions and their resultant cascading. This also brought about the regular use of CC 72000s out of Paris Gare du Nord on workings to Laon.

►The first 'Sybic' loco No. 26001 seen on test at Nevers on 3rd August in the company of 25602. *E. Dunkling*

▼TGV-Atlantique. The trackbed and overbridges were ready for tracklaying near the village of Esvres (close to Tours) when this photograph was taken in August. A massive viaduct will be built near here to span the River Loire. *Michael J. Collins*

EAST GERMANY

In 1988 East Germany finally said farewell to regular main line steam workings. The vast amount of electrification work being done finally made enough diesels spare to allow the last main line steam locos to be laid up. In the spring and early summer the lines in the south east of the country gradually finished using steam and by the 29th October it was all over when 50.3559 worked the official last steam trains. It covered for a diesel on trains between Halberstadt and Magdeburg. Steam still survives on the narrow gauge but not for much longer as the first rebuilt V100 was delivered to the Harz system in December and rumour has it that 30 diesels have been ordered from Romania for the 750 mm gauge lines. Then it really will be the end.

►Standard gauge steam passenger workings still existed in East Germany in 1988. This delightful view of Class 50.35 No. 3556-3 with its vintage coaches was taken at Ochersleben on 1st March. The train is the 12.53 to Gunsleben.
Graham Scott-Lowe

◄The headboard translated into English reads "Last Journey! End of steam loco. services from Glauchau shed with train 56353 from Rochlitz to Glauchau 11–12 June 1988". Class 50.35 2–10–0 No. 3670-2 nears Glauchau on 12th June. *Graham Scott-Lowe*

▼After working the freight referred to above, the 50.35 was put on show at Glauchau depot and is seen in the company of original Class 50 2–10–0 No. 50 849 and Class 86 2–8–2T No. 86 049. *Graham Scott-Lowe*

WEST GERMANY

The main event of 1988 must be the DB's opening of the first section of the *Neubaustrecke* from Fulda to Würzburg, with the bringing into normal service of the Class 120 Bo–Bo electric locomotives. It was not long after the opening of the new line that stories were heard of lots of locos out of service and even carriages stopped for various defects, air conditioning and doors being mentioned. Ordinary toilets caused problems too, caused by the higher air pressure 'outside' in the tunnel! Vacuum toilets are now mandatory!

The locos had various problems, one of which is also associated with tunnels. On moving from dry rails in tunnels onto wet rails outside, wheel slip has been experienced; the on-board computer thinks the train is exceeding the speed limit and applies the brakes. All these problems were quickly tackled but it does show that new technology is not introduced without problems.

Hamburg was the centre of attraction in the summer when the IVA (International Verkehrs Ausstellung) - International Transport Exhibition - was staged. (See separate feature).

The Franco–German rivalry intensified when the world speed record was wrenched from the SNCF's TGV on 1st May when 406.9 km/h was reached on the *Neubaustrecke*.

The summer timetable saw the introduction of one of the longest S-Bahn routes, that from Hagen to Mönchengladbach. There were also several closures, mostly branch lines which had their rail passenger services replaced by buses. The continuing rationalisation of branch line passenger and freight services together with the introduction of more Class 628.2 DMUs had its effect on the motive power fleet.

CLASS WITHDRAWN. The last of the DB's Class 194 locos were finally withdrawn during 1988, although other examples of this class, originally DRG Class E 94 still exist in East Germany (Class 254) and Austria (Class 1020). 194 038-6 is seen at Ingolstadt depot in the company of 194 071-7.
Graham Scott-Lowe

Gone from the scene now are Class 194, 221, and 601, whilst the ranks of Class 211, 515, 815, 798, 998 continue to dwindle. The 798s and 998s will have an extra lease of life as the DB has announced the conversion of some of these to driver-only operation. During the year more shunters of Class 333 and 361 were converted to remote-control operation becoming Class 335 and 365. The new livery appears to be here to stay and examples of most classes have now appeared in the new red. Three Class 141s received the livery being dedicated to work the new IC shuttle service between Mainz and Wiesbaden, one loco at each end of two coaches! Some driving trailers are now to be provided.

The winter timetable brought another new service – InterRegio. These new inter-regional services are to replace the D trains eventually. The first of the new 2 hourly services started operation between Hamburg and Kassel complete with refurbished stock from the Weiden workshops. New-liveried Class 103s were drafted in to Hamburg to work the trains!

DB was another country to test tilting trains. Both the Italian 'Pendolino' and the Spanish 'Talgo Pendular' made visits. It was the second time the Italian train had been tested and DB has now ordered a DMU version of the Pendolino to work services from Nürnberg to Bayreuth/Hof and Stuttgart.

ITALY

Italian technology was tested in Austria and West Germany (qv) but at home the production series of ETR 450 had already finished trial running and were being introduced to traffic before the year end. Routes from Torino to Milano and on to Roma are the first to get the new units. On the Milano–Roma run the 4 hr 55 mins loco-hauled timings have been cut to 3 hr 58 mins with ETR 450s. Other new deliveries included the first of the high speed locos of Class E402 and the first 25 kV loco for Sardinia where the wires are already going up. A few more E633.2 appeared as did the first of a new batch of E656s. Besides the ETR 450s another EMU type, ALe582 was delivered for local services; Sicily was an area to benefit from the latter.

No DMUs are being built or on order and the last main line diesel loco on order was delivered early in the year (D445.1150 delivered February 1988). However, new diesel shunters with three-phase motors are being delivered (Class 145.1, 145.2). Bologna, Reggio Calabria and Messina received batches, amongst other places.

The new deliveries had their effect on older types and by springtime virtually all the Class 2Do2s of Class E428 were out of service. Older types of diesel shunters were also mothballed or sold. The E424s dating from the late 1940s, however, are being refurbished and converted for push-pull operation and now appear in a pleasing new red and grey livery.

FS also looked at its loss-making branch lines and announced a large closure programme which caused an uproar in parliament. There was an even bigger uproar when the scandal of the disposable bed sheets came to light. It appears that a high- ranking FS official placed an order for disposable bed sheets with a family friend. The order was worth some £60 m and covered supplies for some 25 years! The beans were spilt when someone who had offered a supply at a much lower cost complained. The FS board resigned and four officials were arrested. There then followed other scandals about FS officials who have their offices fitted out with extravagant furniture and fittings – again costs were fantastic. Little wonder that branch lines have to struggle!

Permanent way contractors and industrial users continue to buy up second-hand locos from all over Europe with the result that in Italy you can see examples of former DB Classes 211, 216, 220, 260, 261, 265, 323, 324, 601 and 613, SNCB Classes 60 and 80, and NS Class 2400!

During 1988 FS fully commissioned the new marshalling yard at Torino Orbassano which included a new locomotive depot. Pescara got its new station after some 20 years' construction; this also included a new subshed. At Ancona a completely new major locomotive and railcar depot were built north of the old depot.

CLASS WITHDRAWN. Another DB Class to be completely withdrawn during 1988 was Class 221, formerly Class V200.1. 221 149-8, 221 132-4 and 221 116-7 are seen at Oberhausen Osterfeld Sud depot on 28th February. *Mike Goodfield*

NEW ITALIAN STOCK

◀One of the newest electric units in Italy Ale 582 065 built for the lines in Sicily and the far south of Italy on Napoli Campo Flegrei depot on 22nd March.
E. Dunkling

▼Deliveries are nearly complete now of Class D445 diesel locos. D445 1142 is seen on Taranto depot on 25th March.
E. Dunkling

▲One of the newest diesel locos in Italy D145 1014 is seen on Bologna San Donato depot on 19th March. These will replace the ex-USATC D143 class locos currently in use. *E. Dunkling*

LUXEMBOURG

1988 was a quiet year in which electrification of the northern line to Trois Vierges got underway in earnest and modernisation of the main station in Luxembourg continued. During the year CFL took delivery of some new departmental shunters which were immediately put to work on the electrification project. With completion of the project in mind CFL ordered 22 new EMUs from France. These will be based on the SNCF Z2 types.

PORTUGAL

Slow but steady progress continued on the Douro bridge project at Porto. New stainless steel coaches were introduced sporting interiors inspired by SNCF Corail stock. French influence was also shown by the delivery of more Alsthom Class 2600 electric locos. However, the Alsthom diesels based at Barreiro seem to be a disappointment and loco workings had to be amended giving more work to other classes, including the English Electric 1800s. The redistribution of work is believed to be the reason behind the through workings of RENFE Class 333s to Pampilhosa. Finally, towards the end of the year CP decided to buy some surplus diesels from RENFE.

SWEDEN

During what was a year of consolidation the last Rc thyristor loco was delivered. Rc6 1422 was the 360th of Class Rc, a class dating back to 1967. No more locos are on the order books once new high speed EMUs of Class X2 appear. SJ has continued to modernise its carriage fleet continuing the design first introduced in 1981. Some of the displaced carriages will be sadly missed as they were amongst the most comfortable in Europe. Amongst the new coaches were some driving trailers for use on the Stockholm–Uppsala shuttles.

NETHERLANDS 

A year of continued progress with the Flevolijn being extended to Lelystad on schedule. Plan E stock was all withdrawn from service and the Kerkrade–Simpleveld line was closed to passengers. This was an unusual closure as elsewhere in the country the NS has been experiencing terrific growth, so much so that the withdrawn Plan Es are already missed and NS is already thinking about hiring stock from DB or SNCB/NMBS! During 1988 the first of the new diesels of Class 6400 arrived and underwent tests. The tests showed up some problems resulting in the decision to overhaul some Class 2400 diesels that otherwise would have been scrapped.

◀Lelystad Centrum station at platform level with a Sprinter EMU in the platform waiting to leave with a stopping service to Amsterdam. The station is extremely spacious and futuristic in design. *Peter Fox*

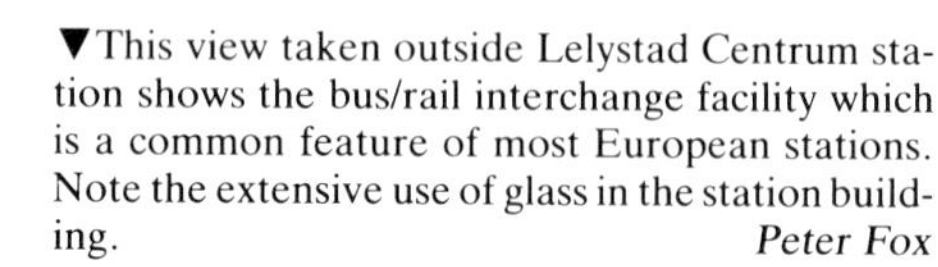

▼This view taken outside Lelystad Centrum station shows the bus/rail interchange facility which is a common feature of most European stations. Note the extensive use of glass in the station building. *Peter Fox*

SPAIN 

Another year of change and progress with many major projects taking place. Construction of the high speed line from Madrid to Cordoba and Sevilla got underway. Madrid Atocha station closed towards the end of the year with the opening of a new station nearby. At Sevilla the first sod was cut and work got underway in constructing a new central station for Sevilla at Santa Justa.

RENFE also got itself a high speed loco by receiving the first rebuilt 269.600 now fitted out for 200 km/h operation. The only other new locos received were the last of an order for 20 shunters of Class 309. However, during the year orders were placed for a fleet of new shunting locos. New Inter City EMUs of Class 444.500 were delivered and tests continued with the prototype suburban EMU of Class 445. Talgo trains were in demand and a 6-car rake went on test in the USA followed by trips to West Germany and Austria where the Pendular Talgo was tested on curvacious routes. As the year closed a RENFE announcement shook the whole of Europe: its new line to Andalucia will be built to standard gauge and other lines will be converted to standard gauge to form a high speed network that will link into the European system. Moreover, RENFE showed its European commitment by placing orders for 24 high speed trains with Alsthom (TGVs!) and 75 high speed electric locos to Siemens (120s!). For the last 20 years or so most electric locos have been of Japanese origin and so it is quite a turnaround.

INTERNATIONAL TRANSPORT EXHIBITION – HAMBURG

IVA 88 (Internationale Verkehrs Ausstellung 88) was the title of an international transport exhibition held in Hamburg from May 1988. The exhibition was held on a large site between Hamburg Dammtor and Sternschanze stations, the former being a station served by IC trains whereas the latter is served only by the Hamburg S-bahn. Most of the British railway press gave scant attention to the exhibition, completely missing the important developments on show, but concentrating almost entirely on the movement of the British large exhibits.

The exhibition was staged in a large centre, with the railway vehicles being shown on a separate site adjacent to Sternschanze station.

The UK was well-represented with a complete hall devoted to the theme 'Britain's new railways'. Leading UK civil, mechanical and electrical engineering companies were exhibiting including Balfour Beatty Ltd., BREL, Brecknell Willis, British Steel, Brush, Davies & Metcalfe, GEC, Hunslet, Plessey, RFS Industries, Westinghouse, the Railway Industries Association and ML Engineering of Plymouth (who were exhibiting a novel fibre optic route indicator for signals).

BR vehicles on show were 89001, 90008, 91003 and 150 263. Unlike most other countries' large exhibits, the British ones were mainly locked, with the public being denied access, but the Class 150 was open on the second occasion on which the author visited the exhibition, albeit with no representative on hand to explain the reasoning behind the cramped seating layout to the German visitors who were generally seen to be falling about laughing and cracking jokes about how small the inhabitants of England must be!

In the author's opinion, pride of place in the exhibition must go to the 'Interregio' stock of the DB and the IC3 DMUs of the DSB (although the latter, along with the BR Class 91 electric loco and the NS Class 6400 diesel loco were to suffer that scourge of the late 1980s, software problems).

The Interregio stock of the DB presented a new concept in rebuilt coaching stock. Old DB coaches had been completely gutted and renovated by a company jointly owned

▲The revolutionary DB Interregio 'Bistro' buffet has an extremely pleasing interior with its circular seating upholstered in green and black, a mixture of direct and indirect lighting and glass table-tops. The bar is also of pleasing design. *Peter Fox*

►Is this coach open or compartment? The DB Interregio first class vehicle has four-seater compartments along one side of the vehicle with pairs of seats in an open layout along the other. Extensive use is made of glass, with compartment doors and luggage racks being mainly glass and large mirrors on compartment bulkheads. *Peter Fox*

▲The revolutionary end design of the Ascan-Scandia IC3 Inter-City DMU for the DSB is seen here in the "driving" position. The whole cross-section is used for the rubber gangway, with the hinged drivers cab module inside it. *Peter Fox*

▼The pleasing interior of a second class coach of an IC3 set. Note the dot matrix information display on the bulkhead. *Peter Fox*

by the DB (51%) and a glass manufacturer. Needless to say, glass plays a large part in the construction of the vehicles interiors, even down to the luggage racks being made from glass! The coaches have been remodelled on extremely spacious lines with a new 'Bistro' catering vehicle concept. The coaches are intended for service on the DB's new Interregio network, a new type of service on routes not served by Intercity trains and which can be compared to BR Provincial's 'Express' routes.

The DSB IC3 is a new design of InterCity diesel multiple unit designed by Ascan Scandia. It features a revolutionary end design in which the entire front end hinges back to reveal a full width through gangway between units. Features for the passengers include a dot matrix passenger information system, five-channel stereo radio at seat with plug-in headphones, video, telephone and fax. Each unit has two power cars and one trailer with a total installed power of 1176 kW. The total weight is 90 tonnes and the maximum speed is 180 km/h.

Another brand new railway coach design was 'WAGGON 2000', built by Simmering–Graz–Pauker AG and Jenbacher Werke AG of Austria. The coach has a futuristic exterior (see photo on page 127) and a spacious interior with both open and compartment areas. Wardrobes are provided and also headphone sockets, but it is difficult to describe the vehicle as particularly innovative. It is designed for 250 km/h, and is 26 metres long, but with a tare weight of 50.5 tonnes it is hardly lightweight.

Other passenger vehicles on display were new DR electric loco 243 354, a modern DR (East German) day coach, an NS double-decker, a DSB EMU, a new Hamburg U-bahn set and a prototype set for the West Berlin S-bahn.

Freight vehicles were also in evidence with both Unilok and Minilok exhibiting bimodal (road/rail) tractors.

Other locomotives on show were DB 120 127-6 and 111 068-3, with a new Class 628.2 DMU running tours to Maschen marshalling yard. The new NS three-phase Class 6400 diesel loco No. 6401 'Mijndert' was also present.

IVA IN COLOUR

▲**The stylish exterior of 'Waggon 2000', the product of Austrian vehicle builders SGP.** *Peter Fox*

▼**This VTG tank wagon speaks for itself!** *Peter Fox*

▲**New prototype vehicles for the West Berlin S-bahn (left) and the Hamburg U-bahn (right). The different loading gauges of the two systems are clearly shown by the sizes of the vehicles.** *Peter Fox*

►**A programme of steam specials was operated in connection with the exhibition using the DB's museum locomotives 01 1100 and 41 360. 01 1100 is seen on 5th June approaching Morsum (Sylt) with the return 'Schimmelreiter' excursion from Westerland (sylt) to Hamburg.** *Peter Fox*

▲The DB's ICE became the world rail speed record holder on 1st May at 406.9 km/h. It is seen at Fulda on 29th May after having worked a demonstration run over the *Neubaustrecke* from Würzburg on 29th May, the first day of public operation over the line. *Peter Calderley*

▼The SNCF's TGV-Atlantique will be the fastest train in the world when full operation begins in September 1989. This will be some eight years after the original TGVs started their regular sprints between Paris and Lyon, revolutionising rail travel between these cities. One of the new sets is pictured here on the new LGV near Dourdon during 1988 proving trials. *P. Ouvain/SNCF Centre Audio-Visuel*

◀New RENFE Inter City/Electrotren unit No. 8444 504-5 stands at Barcelona on the evening of 6th July. The colours of these new units are standard with the latest loco-hauled coaches and the scheme is called 'Estrella'. *Kieran J. Platt*

►Krupp/Mak were showing off their new Class 6400 diesel for the NS. The first of the class, No. 6401 is named 'Mijndert'.
Peter Fox

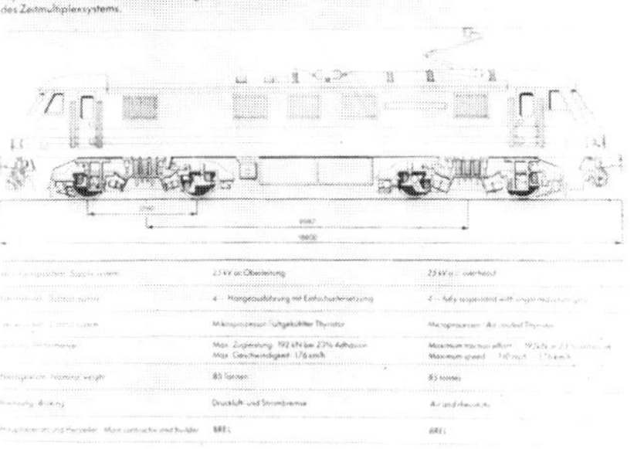

The British displays at the IVA were marketed as "Britain's New Railways". On the left, a typical display stand, this one from the Class 90 locomotive. Note the translation error, *Klasse* for 'Class'. This should be *Baureihe* – *Klasse* means 'Class' as in 'First Class'. A general view of the British exhibits is shown at the bottom of the page, with 150 263 on the left and 89001, 90008 and 91003 on the right. The DB Class 120 can be seen in the distance. Two BR departmental ferry vans (formerly motor car vans) 889009/15 were used to transport ancillary items for BR's exhibits. These are shown below in their special livery.
Peter Fox

A GLIMPSE OF IRELAND

◄Iarnrod Eireann (Irish Rail) has recently acquired three Class 80 DMUs on long term loan from Northern Ireland Railways. One of them (Nos. 737, 761 and 68) is seen leaving Bray on the 11.27 Bray–Arklow service on 18th May. (Normally the unit works between Bray and Greystones only, but this particular working is extended to Arklow and return). The arrival of these units has ended the final push-pull Irish Rail service using converted CIE/Park Royal railcars (Nos. 6107 (driving trailer), 6311 and 6206) and, latterly Class 121 locos. *David Percival*

THE SHANNON RAILTOUR

►The RPSI 'Shannon Railtour' (14th-16th May 1988) was the first outing for their newly-overhauled LMS (Northern Counties Committee) corridor third. No. 241, seen here at Athenry on 15th May. *David Percival*

▼2–6–4T No. 4 storms towards Birdhill (on the Ballybrophy–Limerick line) on a 'run past' on 14th May. *David Percival*

▼►No. 184 is seen at Woodlawn on 15th May. *John Checkley*

A RAILWAY DIARY FOR 1988

JANUARY

2. PRESERVATION. Peak No. D 100 is delivered to Peak Rail at Matlock.
4. CHANNEL TUNNEL. Tunnel boring commences from the English and French coasts just under 2 years since the Anglo-French Fixed Link Treaty was signed (by Margaret Thatcher and François Mitterand on 12/02/86).
4. PRESERVATION. Preserved 'Deltic' No. D 9000 Royal Scots Grey, is transferred to Stewarts Lane depot on the Southern Region for storage.
4. OPENING. Tunstead–Hindlow limestone traffic is inaugurated.
6. STATION CONSTRUCTION. Work starts on the new £400,000 Halewood station, Merseyside. Nearly 10,000 people live within a half-mile radius.
9. NEW STOCK. Class 156 unit No. 156 402 commences a tour of Scotland to show passengers and staff the new type of rolling stock to be introduced – the reception is not favourable.
9. OPENING. A new coal depot is opened at Yeovil Junction.
11. LIGHT RAIL. Metrolink (the Manchester LRT project) tendering – for the design, construction, maintenance and operation – is approved by the government.
11. TRACTION. After more than two decades the Class 03s are finally withdrawn from north eastern operation, with the last Gateshead example, No. 03078 withdrawn.
11. NEW STOCK. The first Class 319 'Thameslink' unit is commissioned at Strawberry Hill for Network South-East. Units are used on various Southern Region routes prior to the Snow Hill Cross-London route opening.
11. TRAINING. Driver training commences on the Western Region with Class 155 Sprinter stock. Training trips are operated from Bristol, Exeter and Plymouth.
11. ELECTRIFICATION. The entire 143 miles between London Waterloo and Weymouth is electrified as from today with the official energisation of the Branksome to Weymouth stretch. A special ceremony is held at Wareham.
11. CATERING. Travellers Fare, the catering arm of British Rail retains 68 out of the 96 of its sites for which tenders were invited.
12. CEREMONY. The Queen officially opens the new rail/air terminal for the Gatwick Express at London's Victoria station.
12. MEDIA EVENT. The press launch of new Class 156 Super Sprinter stock is held at Norwich.
14. PLAN. London Regional Transport's Annual Business Plan for 1988/9 is published. Increased capacity and schemes to remove bottlenecks are high priorities for London Underground Ltd.
15. RE-OPENING. Littlehampton station is re-opened by the chairman of West Sussex County Council. The station was rebuilt at a cost of £600,000.
19. BAD WEATHER. The line to Largs, west of Glasgow, makes the national TV news as part of coverage of the day's appalling weather. A high tide, backed by gale-force winds causes suspension of electric services. EMUs on the coastal sections of the line had been suffering from severe arcing from the salt spray.
20. INVESTMENT. Commenting on the 1988 Public Expenditure White Paper, published today, transport secretary Paul Channon says: "BR plan to spend a £3 billion (at today's prices) over the next 5 years. This represents the biggest rail renewal programme since the transition from steam to diesel".
20. TRACK MAINTENANCE. Dr John Prideaux, InterCity director promises faster journeys, and expects significant track-laying cost savings, following the introduction of 11 dynamic track stabilisers.
21. END OF AN ERA. It is announced that Lickey banking will end from May 1988. The sole-surviving booked banking of a passenger train in recent years has been that of the 21.24 Bristol Temple Meads–Glasgow/ Edinburgh, almost always by one or two Class 37s. From May, the northbound train will originate from two places, Poole and Plymouth, the two halves being joined at Birmingham. The lighter formation from the West Country removes the need for banking.
21. CHANNEL TUNNEL. Mr Malcolm Southgate, director, Channel Tunnel, says that BR will arrange meetings with statutory bodies and organisations by region to maximise benefits from the Channel Tunnel to the whole of Britain. (This is in accordance with the Channel Tunnel Act, Section 40).
23. MOTORWAY CLOSES. The M11 is closed for almost 24 hours to allow construction of the rail bridge to carry part of the new 4-mile Stansted Airport branch over the motorway.
26. NEW WAGONS. Cornish china clay: the first train of CDAs enter revenue-earning service.
26. LONDON UNDERGROUND. Full restoration work begins at King's Cross following the fire.
30. EXTENSION. A Class 127 DMU is the first train to Belgrave on the new extension of the Great Central Railway, Leicestershire.
31. FLOODING. Serious flooding in Higham tunnel on the Rochester line results in diesel haulage, a mixture of Class 33-hauled and DMU-operated services.

FEBRUARY

1. EXHIBITION. The Mail by Rail exhibition at the National Railway Museum is opened.
1. BUSINESS TRAVEL. Passengers with a full-price standard ticket enjoy 'silver standard' service on key business trains between Liverpool and London. As most business travellers are restricted by company policy to using standard class, they will appreciate the complimentary refreshments and at-table service – as offered by airlines' club classes.
1. CATERING. British Rail's new airline-style catering operation, Cuisine

Following several weeks of heavy rain, Strood and Higham Tunnels (on the North Kent line between Gravesend and Rochester) became flooded. Electrical equipment was damaged necessitating diesel working instead until 22nd February. Here, 33113 propels Class 438 '4 TC' 8029 at Higham on a Rochester–Gravesend shuttle on 9th February. *Rodney Lissenden*

2000, is criticised for poor value and poor quality by the North West Transport Users Consultative Committee.
5. CONFERENCE. A major conference, 'The Channel Tunnel: making the Most of Link in the North' is held in Manchester.
7. EXERCISE. British Transport and Metropolitan police forces, fire and ambulance services stage an exercise in dealing with a King's Cross-type accident. The scenario is a serious derailment of a peak-hour train in the tunnels between Drayton Park and Moorgate, with evacuation being complicated by a fire at Essex Road station.
8. RATIONALISATION. On the Wolverhampton–Shrewsbury line, Shifnal, Albrighton, Codsall and Bilbrook become unstaffed stations. Automatic ticket-issuing machines are installed at each, and at the larger Wellington and Telford Central stations. Tickets can also be bought on trains.
9. CHANNEL TUNNEL TRAIN. Following a competition among the best of Europe's specialist designers, the British Railways Board announce the winning team.Consisting of British, French and Belgian designers, it aims to ensure an attractive interior, exterior and livery for around 41 trains, each capable of up to 187 mph. The British company, Jones Garrard of Leicester, responsible for the new train's exterior, was extensively involved with the stylish Class 442 Bournemouth stock's design.
9. DIVERSION. Hurricane K strikes the west coast. Speed restrictions, flooding at Preston and falling trees across the line at Shap on the West Coast Main Line bring another moment of glory for the Settle–Carlisle line.
9. RAILFREIGHT. Final operation of 'Clay Hood' OOV freight wagons from Fowey, Cornwall, replaced by new air-braked BR-owned CDA wagons, constructed at Doncaster.
10. LIGHT RAIL. Greater Manchester PTE LRT bills 1 and 2 receive Royal Assent.
12. TRACTION. Class 91 roll-out at BREL Crewe. Locomotive No. 91001 is handed over from GEC Transportation Projects to BR for operational tests, with the locomotive operating from works for the first time under its own power two days later. The new loco makes its appearance in the well-produced Channel 4 documentary Equinox: 'Running To Time'.
12. CAR SERVICING. The first 'Serviceman' car servicing depot in the South Western sub-sector of the Southern Region is opened at Winchester. Network SouthEast plans similar depots at Basingstoke, Dorking, Milford, Haslemere, Havant and Winchfield. 'Serviceman' depots are planned on or near large commuter car parks at other Network SouthEast stations too.
15. MODERNISATION. The modernised Winnersh station, completed at a cost of £110,000 is opened. Winnersh lies on the Southern Region's Reading–Waterloo/Guildford lines.
17. ROLLING STOCK. The first 3-car Class 150/1 unit formed at Derby Etches Park, by coupling Class 150/2 vehicle between existing Class 150/1 stock.
17. RAILFREIGHT. The first Railfreight-liveried Class 47/4 No. 47599 is outshopped from BREL Crewe, carrying 'Speedlink' sub-sector colours.
21. PRESERVATION. The first steaming occurs of West Country Pacific No. 35027 PORT LINE.
22. ELECTRIFICATION. Through electric services from the West Coast Main Line to East Anglia via the North London line are possible from today.
26. DERAILMENT. Class 37 No. 37138 becomes derailed on the loop at Leiston, on the Saxmundham–Sizewell branch in Suffolk, whilst hauling a fly-ash train. Class 31s Nos. 31282 and 31320 rescue the train while Ipswich staff re-rail the Class 37 and repair damaged track.
26. FOSTER YEOMAN. The contract is signed between Foster Yeoman and GM-EMD for the fifth Class 59 freight locomotive.
29. BARRY SCRAPYARD. The last Barry locomotive is sold; Churchward 2–8–0 No. 2873 has the honour of being the last of the 213 locomotives originally stored at Barry docks to be sold.
29. PRESERVATION. First revenue-earning duty for 'Jinty' 47279 on the Keighley and Worth Valley Railway (KWVR).

MARCH

1. NEW LAYOUT. Work starts on the York station re-modelling scheme, the biggest track remodelling and resignalling (Solid State Interlocking) programme since that at Crewe, in 1985. Costing £18 m and taking 15 months, speeds through York station will be raised from 15 mph to 50 mph.
4. STRIKE ACTION. InterCity and East London suburban services are severely disrupted for 48 hours when Stratford drivers stage an unofficial strike over the disc-braked suburban trains. The union cites many examples of poor braking, particularly two accidents during autumn 1987 at Walton-on-the-Naze and Forest Gate involving Classes 313 and 315 respectively.
5. PRESERVATION. The first through train operates from BR to the Birmingham Railway Museum.
6. DERAILMENT. The locomotive is derailed whilst hauling a vinyl chloride monomer tank train soon after leaving ICI's Hillhouse works on their freight branch just north of Poulton-le-Fylde, Lancashire. The train had been en route to Barry.
6. RESTORATION. The new Ingrow station buildings are formally opened on the KWVR.
9. PASSENGER ENVIRONMENT. Network SouthEast announces a £160 m scheme to clean up its 935 stations over the next 7 years. Property development, improved security, better car-parking, and priority for the 60 busiest stations are key features.
10. NETWORK SOUTHEAST. Network SouthEast announces a £17 m scheme to modernise, and increase seating capacity, on its 768-vehicle fleet of Class 423 (VEP) EMUs British Rail Maintenance at Eastleigh will carry out the 4-year programme.
11. DEMOLITION. An early rail-air interchange, the original Gatwick Airport station – south of the present one – is demolished. The mid-1930s station now gone, only the old airport terminal building and the tunnel between the two sites remain. Shortly afterwards, amidst much publicity, BAA opens its new Gatwick North Terminal, linked to the existing Gatwick South by three-car 'peoplemover' trains.
13. OBITUARY. Sir Henry Johnson, BR chairman from 1968–71, dies aged 81.
13. EXTENSION. Paul Channon inaugurates track-laying of the Bluebell Railway extension to East Grinstead.
14. DOCKLANDS. Work starts on the Bank extension of the Docklands Light Railway. The first stage is scheduled for completion in 1990 and will provide a direct rail link from the heart of the City of London to the huge Canary Wharf office development in particular.
14. PRESERVATION. The preserved Class 503 is finally withdrawn from active service.
17. RE-OPENING. The Mauchline–Annbank line in Strathclyde is reopened by Railfreight Coal.
17. CAMPAIGN. Having been neglected for many years, a publicity campaign is inaugurated for the Bishop Auckland–Saltburn line. Branded the Heritage line, local authorities and other groups are also supporting the campaign.
20. CAMPAIGN. With business and local community support, ScotRail launches 'Operation Springclean' to improve the appearance of stations, the lineside and rolling stock. ScotRail also plans to improve the reliability of 'certain units'.
20. FREIGHT. ECC Quarries are awarded a £200,000 Section 8 grant to enable their depot at Bow, East London, to handle 36 privately-owned hopper discharge aggregate wagons operating from Croft Quarry, Leicestershire.
22. DISABLED TRAVEL. The Earl of Snowdon criticises British Rail's lack of provision for disabled travellers. Citing an example, he said: "It is evidently perfectly acceptable to lock someone in a wheelchair in an unheated, unlit, unattended cage", [the guard's van].
22. NEW PLAN. The Manpower Ser-

vices Commission and the construction company Jarvis announce a £5 m plan to turn the 72-mile Settle–Carlisle line into a tourism corridor. About five major attractions would be needed, spread along the line, possibly including a navvy museum at Ribblehead. The plan, however, depends on a decision on the line's future.

23. JUMBO OIL TRAIN No. 1. 20 x 100-tonne TEA/TEBs are hauled from Immingham to Nottingham.

23. CHANNEL TUNNEL. West Country No. 34016 BODMIN hauls a symbolic first freight train on the Isle of Grain conveying concrete lining segments for the Channel Tunnel.

24. UNIONS. The three rail unions launch their 'Better Rail Campaign'. It is claimed that the one-off cost of £500 m and additional running costs of £137 m would be self-funding, as passenger demand responds to improved punctuality, cleanliness and journey times.

26. OPEN DAY. The first-ever public open-day is held at Bournemouth depot. It is arranged to show off new Class 442 'Wessex Electric' stock. Also featured is LMS Standard Class 5 loco No. 5305.

26. BRML DONCASTER. The final Heavy General Overhaul is completed by BRML Doncaster on Class 31 No. 31106. The locomotive is outshopped in conventional rail blue livery and is operated by the Departmental sector.

26. NEW LIVERY. The first Class 33 to be repainted in Railfreight sub-sector livery, appears when 33205 is outshopped in Railfreight Speedlink colours for 'Train Ferry pool' service.

27. ANNIVERSARY. Twenty five years to the day since the Beeching Report on the future of British Railways was published, Britain's remaining rail network is thriving.

30. LITTER. In a High Court case London Regional Transport is found negligent in failing to remove potentially dangerous litter. The case is brought by a policeman who slipped on a discarded hamburger and broke his leg whilst chasing thieves at Earl's Court station.

30. RESERVATIONS. British Rail announce that all 3,000 accredited travel agents throughout Britain will be able to book seats and sleeper berths directly from BR's computer reservation system – 'Railtrak' – by June.

30. PUBLIC SERVICE OBLIGATION. Paul Channon, secretary of state for transport, states that the maximum allowed on the PSO grant to BR for 1988/9 (Network SouthEast and Provincial sectors only) will be £605 m.

31. SUBSIDY. InterCity rail services receive their final subsidy today, just over 25 years after the Beeching Report first attempted to make the railway system profitable.

APRIL

2. ROAD CONGESTION. On this bank holiday weekend Britain experiences its longest ever traffic jam – 115 miles between Bristol and London on the M4.

4. ELECTRIFICATION. The 'missing link' between Royston and Shepreth Branch Junction (3 miles south of Cambridge) is energised.

4. RAIL LINK. Bradford Chamber of Commerce intensifies its efforts to fight new BR notices to formally close the Wortley curve which, until 1985, allowed trains to bypass Leeds station.

10. OPEN DAY. A public open day is held at Stewarts Lane depot, the star attraction being green-liveried 'Deltic' No. D 9000.

13. SIGNALLING. The Exeter Area resignalling project is formally opened. The signalling centre covers 100 miles and replaces 31 signalboxes.

14. WORLD RECORD. Two Class 442 units 2401 and 2403 cover the 142.75 miles between Waterloo and Weymouth in 1 hr 59 min, 24 sec. The units reach 109 mph, a world 750V third-rail traction record.

14. TGV-FRANCE. The SNCF accepts delivery of the first TGV-Atlantique set from the Alsthom company at a handover ceremony at their Belfort works in eastern France.

15. NEW UNITS. Twenty-two new Class 456 two-car units are approved for Network SouthEast South West inner-suburban services.

16. SPEED RECORD. Class 319 EMUs 319 031 and 319 033 break the record for the London–Brighton run. The 50.7 miles from London Bridge to Brighton are covered in 39 min 15 sec, average speed 77.5 mph. On its return the 8 coach train covers the 50.9 miles between Brighton and Victoria in 38 min 56 sec (78.4 mph).

16. PRESERVATION. The first run of 8F No. 48151 in preservation from Derby to Manchester Victoria occurs. The loco coasts into Manchester with most of its firebars melted.

16. END OF AN ERA. D 200 – 40122 operates on BR for the last time with a special from London Liverpool Street to York. After arrival the locomotive is handed over to the National Railway Museum in a special ceremony.

20. RE-OPENING. Cononley station, south of Skipton, is re-opened to passenger traffic. It was closed on 22nd March 1965.

20. TRACTION. Tenders are invited for the re-engineering of up to 147 HST power cars for life extension.

20. ELECTRIFICATION. BR is given authority to electrify the Portsmouth–Southampton and Portsmouth–Eastleigh routes at a cost of £16.4 m.

22. SECURITY. A £3.5 m scheme to improve passenger security is announced for the London Underground system.

24. RE-OPENING. A new station is opened at Balloch in place of Balloch Central which closed on 23rd April 1988. The station cost £220,000 to build and at an official opening ceremony held on 22nd April, ScotRail Provincial manager, for Strathclyde PTE Services, Mike Rayner, says that over the past five years, ScotRail's commitment to station improvements has been to the tune of £22 m, in conjunction with Strathclyde Council.

25. STATION EXPANSION. British Rail begins discussions, through its property board, with Kent County Council and Ashford District Council about land development at Ashford. This will include a £23 m new international station to serve Channel Tunnel rail traffic.

25. OPENING. Cottingley station, between Morley and Leeds, is opened to passenger traffic.

29. CENTENARY EVENT. LMS 'Jinty' No. 7298 and the Severn Valley Railway's GWR 'Prairie' tank No. 4566 haul passenger trains on Lever Bros' Port Sunlight system as part of their centenary celebrations.

29. NEW REGION. British Rail's newest region, Anglia, is formed. With headquarters in the City of London, it covers lines from Fenchurch Street and Liverpool Street to the fastest-growing area of Britain. Mr John Edmonds is the region's general manager.

29. OPENING. The Rt. Hon. Harold Walker, M.P., opens BR's new electrification fixed equipment maintenance depot at Doncaster. Costing £1 m, the depot has a power control room and is a focal point for maintaining the masts, wires and other equipment along

►The East Coast Main Line lost its sleeping car trains from the start of the summer timetable, so this sight is no more. Class 47 loco No. 47663 waits to depart King's Cross with the ECS to Bounds Green depot during the morning rush hour of 22nd April. All sleeping car trains to the North used London Euston from 16th May. *David Percival*

115 route miles of the East Coast Main Line and the Doncaster to Leeds line.

30. CELEBRATION. The 125th anniversary of Ffestiniog Railway is marked today.

MAY

1. WORLD RECORD. The prototype ICE (InterCity Experimental) train of the German Federal Railways (DB), composed of two power cars, a passenger coach, and an instrumentation coach, reaches 406.9 km/h on the completed section of the Hannover–Wurzburg *Neubaustrecke*, a new world rail speed record.

2. OPEN DAY. Colchester depot in Anglia Region opens its doors to the public, with many classes unusual for the area being exhibited including Class 20s and a Class 58.

4. LONDON UNDERGROUND. The new 1986 prototype stock enters service on the Jubilee Line of the London Underground.

5. ROYAL MAIL. MALLARD works the special Mail by Rail train to York.

5. NEW UNIFORMS. Platform staff try out a range of new clothes in a move which may see 20-year old clothes designs replaced. 150 staff are involved in the trial.

7. DIESEL WEEKEND. On 7th and 8th May, Foster Yeoman Class 59 No. 59001 operates on Severn Valley Railway diesel weekend services, using borrowed air-braked rolling stock from BR.

9. TRAIN FERRY. The 160-metre SNCF train ferry Nord Pas-de-Calais enters service between Dover and Dunkerque. Its introduction has been delayed by both industrial action and by construction difficulties of the new linkspan at Dover. Intended to increase Railfreight competitiveness before the Channel Tunnel opens, up to 50 bogied-wagons can be carried on one crossing.

11. ROYAL RE-OPENING. The Princess Royal officially re-opens Snow Hill Tunnel between King's Cross (Midland) and Blackfriars. The cross-London link was last used for regular passenger trains in 1916.

12. MOVEMENT. GWR 'Manor' No. 7828 goes from the Gloucestershire & Warwickshire Railway to the Gwili Railway via Barry.

14. RE-OPENING. Bedworth station, between Nuneaton and Coventry, is opened to passenger traffic from 16th May, the start of the summer timetable. The original station was closed on 18th January 1965. The first passenger train to stop at Bedworth today is a special charter, the 'Bedworth Boomerang', part of the Bedworth gala day.

14. RAILTOUR. The first HST visits Kingswear, Torbay & Dartmouth Railway, when a special is operated by Hertfordshire Railtours from Derby.

Monday 16th May marks the first day of the new Thameslink services. 319 012 stands at Blackfriars station whilst forming the 14.56 Luton to Purley service with sister unit 319 021. *Michael McGowan*

14. END OF AN ERA. The last loco-hauled 'Rhinelander' arrives from Manchester at Harwich, replaced in the new timetable by a Blackpool–Harwich Class 156 Sprinter.

14. ANNIVERSARY. To mark the tenth anniversary of the founding of the Wymondham and Dereham Rail Action Committee, a special train runs from Dereham to Peterborough and the Nene Valley Railway. Over 5,000 people have now been carried on the freight-only branch since the WyDRAC was formed.

15. PROVINCIAL. The final diagrammed Class 33s are used on the Portsmouth–Bristol–Cardiff route, to be replaced by Class 155 Sprinter stock.

16. NEW LINK. The Windsor Link is opened for traffic facilitating north-south journeys via Manchester.

16. RE-OPENING. A new hourly service starts today, financed by South and West Yorkshire PTEs, from Sheffield to Leeds via the Dearne Valley. Two new stations at Goldthorpe and Thurnscoe are opened by South Yorkshire PTE which supports services in the South Yorkshire area. Support also applies to Bolton-on-Dearne station from today.

16. RE-OPENING. Halewood station is re-opened to passenger traffic for the first time in 37 years since it closed on 10th September 1951. Trains will serve the newly-opened station with westbound (Manchester Oxford Road–Hunts Cross service) and eastbound services alternating between Warrington Central and Manchester Oxford Road.

16. RE-OPENING. Lostock station is re-opened. The station is served by trains on the Manchester Victoria–Preston route and is situated just north of Lostock Junction, where the Wigan line diverges. The original station, called Lostock Junction, closed on 7th November 1966.

16. BOUNDARY CHANGE. Support for Sheffield–Barnsley–Huddersfield service is extended from Penistone to be contiguous with South Yorkshire/West Yorkshire boundary. This eliminates British Rail support for the service.

16. CONTRACT. 33050/1 are named at Grain, marking a new contract with Trans Manche Link. No. 33050 becomes 'Isle of Grain' and No. 33051 becomes 'Shakespeare Cliff'.

16. NEW TIMETABLE. British Rail introduces several earlier trains to London for business travellers and a new sleeper service between the south coast, Thames Valley and Glasgow/Edinburgh Pullman services from London to Chester, the West Country, Stratford-Upon-Avon, and the Peak District tap the summer tourist market.

16. SETTLE–CARLISLE LINE. The minister for public transport, David Mitchell, tells Parliament that the government is 'minded' to consent to closure of the Settle–Carlisle line but is deferring a final decision pending a further report from the TUCCs on bus-substitution and passenger hardship.

16. NEW SERVICE. The new Dover–Manchester Travelling Post Office train is introduced.

16. NEW LINE SPEED. The first 140 mph speed indicator boards are erected on the East Coast Main Line for testing of the Class 91. Apart from four 135 mph boards, the new speed applies between Werrington Jn. near Peterborough and the portals at Stoke Tunnel south of Grantham. A signalling modification in the form of a flashing green light is used.

16. NEW SERVICE. A direct Coventry to Nottingham service is introduced,

The new summer timetable saw many changes, particularly to Provincial's services. One success story was the new Nottingham–Coventry service. Here, 150 112 passes Bedlam Lane level crossing (between Nuneaton and Coventry) with the 07.40 Derby–Coventry. Bedlam Lane crossing signalbox was abolished during November 1988 with closure of the road.
Steve Turner

On 16th May, Liverpool Lime Street was host to trains old and new. From left to right are: 304 010 with the 09.47 to Crewe; Class 85 loco No. 85025; 156 411 with the 09.35 to Norwich; 142 064 with the 09.20 to St. Helens Central; Class 47 loco No. 47366 'The Institution of Civil Engineers'; and finally, 150 254 with the 09.15 to Preston.
Doug Birmingham

the journey between the two cities taking 80 minutes.

16. NEW SPRINTER SERVICES. Metro-Cammell-built Class 156 Super Sprinters replace locomotive-hauled East Anglia–Northwest and Leyland-built Class 155s are used on Portsmouth–Cardiff services.

17. SHARE ISSUE. The Severn Valley Railway launches a £500,000 share issue to fund construction of a boiler works at Bridgnorth.

17. RAILFREIGHT. An official contract for the construction of 100 Class 60 Railfreight locomotives is placed with Brush, Loughborough. The first locomotive is due for delivery in 1989.

18. NEW FREIGHT FACILITIES. 37423 is named Sir Murray Morrison, after the pioneer of the British aluminium industry, at Lochaber as new British Alcan facilities are unveiled. The 10-year contract involves the movement of 94,000 tonnes of alumina from Blyth to Fort William.

19. LAST TRAINS. Last day in service of 1938 stock on the London Underground.

19. NEW SIGNALLING. David Mitchell, minister for public transport, officially commissions a new radio signalling system for the West Highland line – 180 route miles are controlled from one signalling centre at Banavie, replacing 16 signalboxes. The RETB scheme has cost £1.85 m.

20. RE-OPENING. The chairman of British Rail re-opens Great Malvern station after a fire caused £100,000 of damage in April 1986.

20. NEW SIDINGS. Two more Redland Rooftiles sidings are opened at Tiverton Junction and Cardiff Tidal.

21. HAMBURG '88. A special train is operated from the Derby Railway Technical Centre to Dover, en route to Hamburg; it is formed of 47561, 89001, 90008, 91003, ADB 889009, 150 263, ADB 889007, BREL 99520 and BREL 99523.

22. SUNDAY TRAIN. A scheduled Sunday train service is provided on the Sheffield–Barnsley–Huddersfield line for the first time in many years.

22. RE-OPENING. British Rail re-opens Stanhope station, County Durham, for a Sunday service from Darlington to Stanhope. The service will run until 2nd October. The branch served Wearhead until 1953 (freight until 1961) and Westgate in Weardale (closed to freight in 1968) but was cut back to Eastgate where there is a Blue Circle Cement works, the source of the rest of its freight traffic. Two councils and the Heritage Line Group have contributed some £9,000 towards initial station improvements.

22. PRESERVATION. Standard 4MT 2–6–4T No. 80080 works a railtour from Nottingham to Matlock.

22. BIRTHDAY HONOURS. Photographers pay for No. 2857 to haul demonstration freights on its 70th birthday on the Severn Valley Railway.

23. RECONSTRUCTION. Work starts on the contruction of a new Guildford station, together with a 50,000 sq. ft. office block on adjacent land.

26. TRAVEL RECORD. Rail Riders club member Andrew Kendall, 15, from Moreton in the Wirral wins BR's Young Super Traveller of the Year Award. During 1987 he travelled 109,885 miles by train.

27. SPEECH. Acknowledging the important role of the Docklands Light Railway, secretary of state for transport Mr Paul Channon, speaking in London, says "Good transport is essential if the inner cities are to attract the businesses that create jobs".

28. OPEN DAY. Bedford station yard holds its open day.

29. NEW LINE. The first service trains operate over the Fulda–Würzburg *Neubaustrecke* in West Germany.

29. OPEN DAY. 29th and 30th May 'Woking 150' exhibition is held at Woking. This is the largest display of traction and rolling stock shown in 1988. Exhibits include six ex-SR steam locomotives.

30. DELTIC. Severe fire damage afflicts No. 55009 on the North Yorkshire Moors Railway.

JUNE

1. EXHIBITION. Held over almost

two weeks, the International Transport and Traffic Exhibition (IVA) in Hamburg. The British theme is: 'Value for money investment in the world's most cost-effective railway'.
Major exhibitors include Germany, Britain, Austria, Denmark and the Netherlands.

2. KING'S CROSS. The 134-acre station redevelopment scheme, Europe's biggest inner city project is given the go-ahead. It will feature a new concourse linking King's Cross with St. Pancras and a new low-level International station as a Channel Tunnel interchange.

2. DERAILMENT. A cement train is derailed at Cupar, Fife, destroying some 1000 m of track and badly damaging a road bridge. Services are diverted via Perth for the next two days, giving the single track line between Perth (Hilton Junction) and Ladybank new importance.

3. PRESERVATION. No. 7828 ODNEY MANOR enters traffic on the Gwili Railway in Dyfed.

4. FAILURE. LMS 'Jubilee' 4–6–0 No. 45593 KOLHAPUR fails at Keighley on a main line steam special and is rescued by No. 25059 of the KWVR.

5. OPEN DAY. The annual railfair at Coalville freight centre is staged. Many visiting locomotives with freight train run-pasts are arranged.

6. RAILWAY SALE. Tenders are invited for the Vale of Rheidol narrow-gauge railway in mid-Wales. British Rail owns the 12 mile steam-operated tourist railway but sees it as an anomaly.

7. DESPERATION. The government commissions Lazard Brothers to find a buyer for the Settle–Carlisle line. A prospectus is issued.

7. ELECTRIFICATION. In a campaign that has gathered momentum, MPs and 30 local councils meet to discuss the hoped-for complete electrification of the London–Sheffield–Leeds line.

8. CRIME. British Rail launches a station poster campaign aimed at reducing fraudulent travel which is estimated to cost £30–40 m per year.

10. TOTAL ROUTE MODERNISATION. Network SouthEast selects the Chiltern Line from Marylebone to Aylesbury and High Wycombe for a £50 m package of improvements to signalling, stations and track. A new maintenance depot to service the new fleet of 'Networker Turbo' DMUs and property development at Marylebone are part of the plan.

15. BREL. A plan to make 1000 workers redundant at Derby is withdrawn, following an increase in workload.

19. RE-OPENING. Falls of Cruachan station is opened for an experimental period until 2nd October 1988. This will serve the Ben Cruachan power station which is very popular with visitors.

20. POLICY. The government acknowledges for the first time publicly that it is considering the privatisation of British Rail.

21. APPOINTMENT. BR appoints Chris Lewin (co-ordinator, private capital) to project manager responsible for overseeing the sale of the Settle–Carlisle line.

24. LONDON UNDERGROUND. The 3-month inquiry into the King's Cross Underground fire ends with the warning that a disaster could happen again.

24. PRESERVATION. North British 0–6–0 No. 673 MAUDE has its first outing on the Bo'ness and Kinneil Railway for TV.

25. PRESERVATION. No. 48151 becomes the first 8F to travel over the Settle and Carlisle route for 20 years.

27. RAILFREIGHT. A new siding opened at Heck on the East Coast Main Line for Plasmor's new automated block production plant.

27. NETWORK SOUTHEAST. Fifty five train services a day are cancelled indefinitely on the south central area due to staff shortages, particularly drivers at London Bridge, Streatham Hill and Selhurst depots and guards at Norwood and Horsham.BR blames property prices for the inability to attract railmen to the South East.

27. ACCIDENT - FRANCE. Fifty nine people die as two suburban trains collide at the low-level suburban station at Gare de Lyon, Paris.

28. ACCIDENT. The Forders Sidings–Cricklewood refuse train becomes derailed just north of St. Albans station. The empty freight train strikes the 20.33 Three Bridges–Bedford EMU, the driver of which is injured. The Up Slow line is particularly badly damaged.

28. DERAILMENT. In the early hours of today, the previous evening's 19.40 Garston–Dagenham Ford's train becomes derailed blocking the Up line near Dagenham Dock station. Single line working over the Down line is necessary through the morning peak until 12.30.

29. LAST TRAIN. The last revenue-earning train runs on the Radstock branch, hauled by 47370.

JULY

3. MUSEUM EXPANSION. The National Railway Museum at York announces a £5 m expansion project. The scheme involves linking the main building with the annexe by an underpass under Leeman Road.

3. SPECIAL RUN. The Class 89, No. 89001 enters booked passenger service when diagrammed for the MALLARD 50th anniversary special between King's Cross and Doncaster. MALLARD takes over from Doncaster to Scarborough.

4. ENERGISATION. From today the entire 186-mile route between London King's Cross and Leeds is energised.

4. ABBEY FLYER. The Network SouthEast route between Watford Junction and St. Albans Abbey is energised at 25 kV, electric service commencing on 11 July.

5. RESIGNALLING. Sir Robert Reid, chairman of the BRB, unveils a plaque at Lancing Signal Box to commemorate completion of the Portslade–Angmering resignalling scheme. The £3 m project involves removal of semaphore signals and 8 signal boxes, with replacement by MAS & CCTV-controlled level crossings, all controlled from Lancing.

5. REGAINED TRAFFIC. Kincardine Power Station regains rail traffic after a six year gap.

6. BR ANNUAL REPORT (1987–8). Demand is buoyant in all sectors for the BR Group. An £82 m loss last year is transformed into a surplus of £291 m. Overall, BR operated well over 20,000 m passenger miles, a rise of 8% 1986–7 and the best year since 1961. BR's chairman, Sir Robert Reid admits that overcrowding is rife and must be cured by new investment.

8. CLOSURE. Rowntree's Halt is closed due to poor patronage. Withdrawal of services will also save the cost of renewing Burton Lane Junction where the branch leaves the Scarborough line.

9. LAST NEWSPAPER TRAINS. 150 years of railway tradition ends with the last news trains running. At Manchester Victoria, just 2 trains replace 12 services and will be for parcels and associated traffic. News traffic has gone to road and air.

12. FIRST RUN. The first revenue earning train for a Class 90 occurs when 90003 powers the 13.40 Blackpool North to Euston. Class 86 No. 86413 is attached in case of failure.

12. POLICY PROPOSAL. The North of England Regional Consortium (a grouping of Northern local authorities established in 1981) calls for an expansion of (rail-served) regional airports in preference to further expansion in the SE, and also again highlights the required minimum investment programme necessary in associated rail infrastructure if people and industry in the North are to enjoy the benefits of the Channel Tunnel.

12. RE-OPENING. Outwood station is opened by West Yorkshire PTE. The trains which will serve this new station are the Scunthorpe–Doncaster–Leeds and Sheffield–Leeds local services.

14. CHANNEL TUNNEL. Having authorised £589 m of investment on existing routes and the new Waterloo terminal, BR hopes to cope with up to 15 m passengers a year until early in the next century. Looking further ahead, BR presents four options for a high-speed tunnel link and three options for a second London terminal – Stratford,

White City and King's Cross.

▲The unique Class 89, No. 89001 passes Harringey, north London, with the 09.00 King's Cross to Scarborough special on 3rd July. For the record, some enthusiasts have branded this fine machine the 'ant-eater'. Less appropriately perhaps, the two other newcomers, Clases 90 and 91 have been nicknamed 'Skodas' and 'Skips' respectively! *Ken Brunt*

15. CLASS 89. No. 89001 commences operation on the 07.00 Peterborough–King's Cross and 17.36 return service. The train is formed of HST stock with an HST power car to provide three-phase power.
15. LAST TRAIN. The last train runs to Shrewsbury Abbey oil terminal.
17. OPENING. The new ticket hall at London Liverpool Street is opened.
17. COMMISSIONING. Sentinel four-wheeled gear-drive system loco 'Departmental No. 54' is formally commissioned at Middleton Railway Centre, Leeds.
18. INTERCITY. InterCity On Board Services announce that cigarettes and cigars will no longer be sold on InterCity trains.
19. BR CORPORATE PLAN. A profit on railway activities of £940 m in the period 1988–93, manpower reductions (by 8,800 to a total of 130,000 employees), continuing reductions in the PSO grant and high investment are key features of the plan.
20. AIRPORT LINK. Paul Channon, secretary of state for transport, approves BR's participation in a joint venture with BAA plc for a fast direct rail link between Heathrow and Paddington at a cost of £190 m. This scheme, recommended in the Heathrow Surface Access Study, was chosen in preference to four others, including an upgrading of the existing Piccadilly line.
26. NEW MINISTER. Michael Portillo replaces David Mitchell as minister for public transport as part of a government reshuffle. A rising star in the Conservative party, he has already been a government whip and personal secretary to the secretary of state for transport.
26. LANDSLIP. The wettest July in 50 years contributes towards the landslip at Dore, 1 mile north of Moreton-in-Marsh on the Cotswold line. The 40 ft high embankment collapses, it taking 2 weeks and £100,000 to re-open the line.
28. NEW LINE. Following the joint decision of SYPTE and InterCity to pay for a new curve at Swinton on the Doncaster to Sheffield route, BR publishes a formal notice proposing the withdrawal of passenger train services between Mexborough East Junction and Aldwarke Junction. The curve will be completed in 1990, as will the new station at Swinton.
28. ELECTRIFICATION A 'Golden Pot' ceremony is held at Fareham, when Michael Portillo, Minister of State for public transport, laid the first conductor rail pot on the Portsmouth–Eastleigh electrification project.
29. LONDON UNDERGROUND. A new managing director, Denis Tunnicliffe, is appointed for London Underground Ltd.
29. TICKETS. The last 'old-fashioned' Edmondson-style ticket is issued on the Southern Region, a 60p standard single from South Merton to Wimbledon Chase. From today APTIS and PORTIS reign supreme.

▲Michael Portillo, MP, was appointed minister for public transport on 26th July. Mrs Thatcher regards him as one of her better 'communicators'. *Department of Transport*

AUGUST

5. SLADE GREEN. Southern Region announce their intention to service their fleet of new Networker trains at a modernised Slade Green Depot from mid-1990.
8. SETTLE–CARLISLE LINE. Lazard Bros. issues a 42 page brochure on behalf of BR providing background information to any prospective purchaser. Details of staffing, structures, associated councils, operating terms and conditions are included. Meanwhile objections to closure (handled by the NW & NE TUCCs) have risen to 32,500.
10. ELECTRIFICATION. First electric passenger service to Leeds. Class 89 No. 89001 hauls the 08.20 King's Cross–Leeds and 12.00 return service.
11. LOCOMOTIVES. The first Class 91 No. 91001 reaches Leeds under electric power; the train is formed of Mark 3 sleeping stock and test car RDB 975422 'Prometheus'.
12. NEW MARKET. Contracts are signed for 'The Travelling College' - the world's first rail-based educational service. The 13 coach train will provide intensive week-long field study courses with computer-equipped classrooms, a kitchen, a recreation coach and dormitory accommodation for 168 students, 16 teachers and 6 BR staff on board.
15. OPENING. Overpool station is opened. Situated between Ellesmere Port and Little Sutton (on the Helsby–Chester via Hooton route), the station cost £70,000 to build.
16. TRACTION. The first of West Yorkshire PTE Class 155s are released from Leyland, painted in WYPTE cream and red livery.
17. LONDON UNDERGROUND. The rebuilding of Angel station on the Northern line is announced.
17. OPEN DAY. Laira depot, Plymouth, holds its public open-day, large crowds attend, but the display is disappointing, with very few visiting locomotives.
24. STAFF SHORTAGES. No fewer than 28 services on the Victoria–Gatwick rail-air link are cancelled today due to staff shortages.
27. RAIL EVENT. A special 'Rail Event' is held at London Bridge station. There is a large display of traction and rolling stock, and many trade stands. 35028 CLAN LINE is in attendance.
30. LAST TRAIN. The last sand train from Oakamoor, Staffordshire, operates today.

SEPTEMBER

3. OPEN DAY. A small public display is staged at Margate station, the main attraction being preserved green 'Deltic' No. D 9000.
5. CHANNEL TUNNEL. Work starts on the running tunnels at Shakespeare Cliff.
6. PRESERVATION. BR-owned Class 40 No. 40135 becomes (probably) the last Class 40 to operate under its own power on BR tracks when it works from Tyseley to Vic Berry's, Leicester, for asbestos removal. The locomotive is scheduled for preservation at Bury.
9. SPEECH. Speaking about the Channel Tunnel, Michael Portillo, minister of state for transport, tries to reassure Northern businessmen: "Regional disadvantages ... are likely to be reduced. Manufacturers in the Midlands and North will no longer be competing in continental markets with one hand tied behind their backs".
11. OPEN DAY. The first open day is held at Kilmarnock.
12. EMIGRATION. LNER Pacific No. 4472 FLYING SCOTSMAN leaves for an extended visit to Australia.
14. VISIT. HRH Prince Charles visits

Birmingham Snow Hill and is shown around the new station by BR officials, including LM Region general manager Cyril Bleasdale. Prince Charles then rides on the footplate of 7029 'Clun Castle' to the Birmingham Railway Museum.

15. ASHFORD INTERNATIONAL. The British Railways Board invites development proposals for 140 acres of its land centreing on the proposed international station at Ashford, next to the existing station. Most of the land is to the south of the station.

15. NEW STOCK. The first Class 321 unit is handed over from BREL York to Network SouthEast in a special ceremony at York Works. It will operate out of London Liverpool Street.

17. CEREMONY. Lostock station, open since 16th May and situated on the Manchester Victoria–Bolton line, is officially re-opened.

18. OPEN DAY. BRML Eastleigh stages an open day to mark the 150th anniversary of London and South Western Railway.

19. REFURBISHMENT. Refurbished Mark 3 sleeper coaches are put on show at Glasgow Central station.

19. PUBLICITY. Class 4MT No. 80080 makes a press run to Sherborne (ecs to Yeovil).

19. INTERCITY. Class 90 locomotive diagrams begin on passenger services.

19. OPENING. The Secretary of State for Trade and Industry, Lord Young of Graffham officially opens Eurotunnel's £2 m Exhibition Centre at St. Martin's Plain, Folkestone.

21. DELTIC. One of No. 55015's engines is replaced at Butterley.

22. PRESERVATION. Publicity steaming of No. 45596 BAHAMAS occurs at Dinting.

23. ORDER. BREL wins an order for 42 International passenger coaches for Indian Railways. The deal is worth £20 m.

24. RAIL EVENT. A two day Rail Event starts at Winchfield, with many side shows. The first day features a run-past freight train and locomotive displays. On the second day a small static display is arranged.

26. NEW LOOK. The £30 m modernisation scheme that is underway on Manchester's rail network reaches a peak from today until the 16th October. Focus of the improvements is the area around Manchester Piccadilly. Services are interrupted while engineers modernise the 30-year-old signalling and complicated track work. The simplified layout is so that rail services can take full advantage of the Windsor Link, fully opened in May 1988.

30. RE-OPENING. Martin's Heron station is re-opened at a cost of £600,000. It is situated on the Reading–Waterloo line.

30. SETTLE–CARLISLE LINE. The Joint Councils and Railway Development Society urge the TUCCs to press BR and the government to withdraw the Settle-Carlisle closure proposal as it was "fatally flawed" and could lead to legal action in the High Court.

OCTOBER

1. RAIL EVENT. A special Network day is organised with a large display of locomotives and rolling stock at Waterloo, including the first steam loco to return to Waterloo since 1967, and a Class 59.

1. OPEN DAY. BRML Wolverton stages a public open day. A Class 90 is put on display, and visitors are able to inspect some of the Royal Train stock.

1. RE-OPENING. Arlesey station is re-opened to passenger traffic for the first time since 1959. The new station cost £630,000 and is served by King's Cross–Peterborough commuter trains. It lies between Biggleswade and Hitchin.

2. RE-OPENING. The Cynon Valley line is re-opened to passenger traffic after 24 years of freight-only status. The £1.9 m cost of re-opening the 7-mile route is met by Mid-Glamorgan County Council. Six new stations along the line will be served by Class 150 Sprinters. The re-opened stations are: Abercynon North, Penrhiwceiber, Mountain Ash, Fern Hill, Cwmbach, Aberdare.

2. CLOSURE. Rotherham Masborough station is closed to passenger traffic due to the re-opening of Rotherham Central in May 1987. The remaining Sheffield–York local service is diverted via Rotherham Central.

2. REFURBISHMENT. Work commences on £200,000 refurbishment and new car park project for Mexborough Station.

2. NEW SIGNALLING. The £4.7 m programme to modernise the 135-mile Cambrian route from Shrewsbury (Sutton Bridge Junction) to Aberystwyth and Pwllheli reaches a critical stage with the commissioning of the RETB signalling system. The one surviving 'signalbox' is at Machynlleth.

2. CLOSURE. Cricklewood depot closes, its maintenance work being tranferred to Selhurst.

3. OPENING. Musselburgh station is opened today. Completed at a cost of £366,000, it is served by the Edinburgh–North Berwick DMU service.

3. LONDON UNDERGROUND. The Bakerloo line enjoys an increased service frequency as from today.

3. INTERCITY. Bradford's InterCity services are switched from Interchange station to Forster Square.

3. IMPROVED SERVICE. Class 156 Super Sprinters are introduced to four through services a day between Newcastle and Glasgow/SW Scotland. Some trains are named: for example the 07.00 Girvan–Newcastle is the 'Tyne Trader'.

3. LOCOMOTIVES. Class 47/4s are diagrammed for use on Waterloo–Exeter service for the first time. All locomotives are allocated to Laira.

6. CRIME. Thieves steal signalling cable in the York area bringing chaos to rail services. Engineers clamp points and use hard signals through York.

8. PRESERVATION. Sentinel No. 54 hauls trains on the North Yorkshire Moors Railway.

9. OPEN DAY. An open day is held at Bescot Yard attracting large crowds. Good displays are put on.

11. CHANNEL TUNNEL. At the Conservative party conference in Brighton, Mr Paul Channon, secretary of state for transport, announces that BR will invite private sector development of a high speed Channel Tunnel link.

11. LONDON UNDERGROUND. Following the King's Cross Underground disaster, in which 31 people died, verdicts of accidental death are recorded.

13. SETTLE–CARLISLE LINE. Engineers revise repair costs for Ribblehead Viaduct to £2.7 m. This compares with £4.3 m in 1986 and £6 m in 1981!

15. PRESERVATION. Class 55 'Deltic' No. 55019 is moved to the Great Central Railway from the North Yorkshire Moors Railway.

15. CLOSURE. From 16.30 today the freight line from Trafford Park Junction (Manchester) to Gorton Junction is closed.

17. SHARE ISSUE. Peak Rail launches its £250,000 share offer to finance the first stage of its plans to re-open the line from Matlock to Buxton. The estimated total cost, to be spread over 15 years, is £2 m. Local councils have all approved the scheme.

18. CLOSURE PLAN. BR announce plans to withdraw passenger services between Gainsborough Trent Junction (Lincs) and Wrawby Junction, Barnetby (Humberside). This forms part of the Sheffield–Retford–Cleethorpes line, i.e. the main line of the former Manchester, Sheffield and Lincolnshire Railway.

20. SIGNALLING. RETB signalling is introduced on the Shrewsbury–Aberystwyth/Pwllheli line.

20. EXTENSION. The Metro subcommittee of Tyne and Wear PTA approve a £10 m extension of the Metro system to Newcastle International Airport. A bill will be presented to Parliament.

22. RE-OPENING. Network SouthEast's 938th station is How Wood, situated on the St. Albans Abbey–Watford branch. The £81,000 cost has been shared between Network SouthEast, Hertfordshire County Council and St. Stephens Parish Council.

26. PRESERVATION. Class 10 No.

D 4092 is moved to the South Yorkshire Railway.
27. LIGHT RAIL. Sheffield's 'Supertram' Line 1 bill receives Royal Assent.
28. LAST JOURNEY. The last ballast train runs from Blodwell, in Shropshire.
28. FEASIBILITY STUDY. Swansea City Council agrees to contribute towards a feasibility study into a restoration of the oldest passenger railway in the world, the Mumbles Railway, along Swansea Bay.
28. DERAILMENT - NORTH LONDON. Class 31 Nos. 31202/226 run away from Cricklewood and derail onto the North Circular Road/M1 interchange at Staples Corner. No. 31202 is broken up on site whilst No. 31226 is rerailed and taken to Stratford for assessment and is later withdrawn.
28. RE-OPENING. Midline services between Redditch and Lichfield station are experimentally extended to the renovated Trent Valley High Level station.
31. RE-OPENING. The Central Wales line between Shrewsbury and Swansea re-opens following the rebuilding of Glanrhyd Bridge.
31. VALLEYS SERVICE. Weekly passenger revenues on Valleys–Cardiff trains reach £145,000, 22% up on 1987.

Five days before the official re-opening of the Swansea–Shrewsbury line, a ballast train, hauled by 37146, became the first train to use the new Glanrhyd bridge. The train was working from Llandeilo Junction Yard to Llandovery on 26th October. The train made several moves back and forth across the bridge for test purposes. The original bridge was destroyed in October 1987 following severe flooding. A Swansea–Shrewsbury DMU fell into the swollen river as a result with the loss of three lives.
Tom Clift

NOVEMBER

1. NEW ORDER. BREL (1988) Ltd. wins a £28 m order from Strathclyde PTE for twenty two three-car Class 320s to operate Glasgow-area local services. The Scottish Office is offering financial assistance.
1. NEW ORDER. BR orders 25 Provincial Express vehicles of Class 158 from BREL (1988) Ltd. This brings the total ordered to 229 vehicles of this type at a cost of £80 m.
1. LONDON UNDERGROUND. The first public telephones at underground level are installed at Victoria, District Line.
1. COLLECTIVE BARGAINING. BR tells the rail unions that it wants to discontinue national pay bargaining and to negotiate on a more regional basis instead.
4. NEW STOCK. The final Class 319. No 319 060 of original order is commissioned at Strawberry Hill and allocated to Selhurst.
10. LONDON UNDERGROUND. The Fennell report investigating the King's Cross Underground disaster is made public almost a year after the tragic event. Dr Tony Ridley, chairman of London Underground Ltd, resigns as a result.
11. PRESERVATION. An agreement is reached between Port Line Loco Project and the Southern Steam Trust for No. 34027 and No. 35027 to go to Swanage for 25 years.
12. ACCIDENT. The driver is killed and 12 passengers are injured when a Class 150/2 Sprinter is derailed and hits a bridge upright at St. Helens Central station, Merseyside.
12. INCIDENT. ETHEL 2 catches fire while being worked southbound over the Settle–Carlisle line. 8F 48151 is in charge of the 'Cumbrian Mountain Express' at the time. The severely-damaged ETHEL 2 is later taken to Glasgow St. Rollox works for repair.
14. APPOINTMENT. Mr Richard Rosser is voted general secretary (elect) of the third biggest rail union, the 40,000-strong Transport and Salaried Staffs Association. He succeeds Mr Bert Lyons.
15. EXPANSION. A £1 m share issue for the West Somerset Railway is launched.
15. JUMBO OIL TRAIN No. 2. 28 x 100-tonne tanks are hauled from Port Clarence to Long Eaton.
16. LONDON UNDERGROUND. A 'graffiti proof' train is unveiled on the East London Line.
16. OPENING. The Kronospan siding at Chirk is commissioned. The sidings lie just north of Chirk station on the Wrexham–Shrewsbury line.
23. OPENING. A £3 m ticket hall is opened at Tower Hill station, on London Underground's District line.
23. DAMAGE. A 3,500 ton Swedish freighter, M.V. Samo, en route to Howden collides with the Goole Swing Bridge, Humberside, damaging the main horizontal section. All trains are diverted via Selby. Damage is estimated at £1 m.
24. STATION PLANS. King's Cross station proposals are unveiled.
30. SETTLE–CARLISLE LINE. Twenty eight MPs from all the main parties submit separate petitions to Parliament with a sum of 80,000 signatures concerning retention of the Settle–Carlisle line.
30. COLLISION. Class 43 No. 43047 on the 16.00 King's Cross–Aberdeen collides with 43087 on the 14.52 Aberdeen–King's Cross on the King Edward Bridge, Newcastle-upon-Tyne.

DECEMBER

2. UNIONS. BR advises the unions that it intends to pay special allowances (up to £10 pw) to the 20,000 staff working within 40 miles of central London. This is aimed at a greater staff retention.
3. FIRST RUN. 'Jinty' No. 47383 and MR Class '1F' No. 41708 take the inaugural train to Harman's Cross on the Swanage Railway.
6. SETTLE–CARLISLE LINE. TUCCs reiterate their 1986 report with a strongly-recommended retention of the Settle–Carlisle line.
6. APPOINTMENT. Mr Brian Burdsall is appointed as British Rail's first director of quality. He will plan the training programmes needed to change staffs attitudes at all levels to delivering a quality service to customers.
8. APPOINTMENT. Mr Don Heath is appointed director, projects, to oversee the bulk of British Rail's £3.8 billion investment programme over the next five years. The principal projects covered are completion of East Coast Main Line Electrification, King's Cross redevelopment, the Channel Tunnel terminal at Waterloo, and Liverpool Street redevelopment and resignalling.
12. COLLISION. The 06.14 Poole–Waterloo (starting at 06.30 from Bournemouth) collides with the rear of the stationary 07.18 Basingstoke–Waterloo in Clapham Cutting. The wreckage is hit by a southbound ECS from Waterloo. Thirty-five people die in the accident.
12. SIGNALLING. The 55-year-old

▲Work started on track remodelling at York in March but disruption to certain services continued all year, particularly at weekends. The station avoiding lines saw heavy use on such occasions. On 11th September, HST power cars 43111 and 43064 ease the 10.55 Newcastle–King's Cross past Yard South. At Holgate Junction the train reversed back into the station. *B.J. Nicolle*

signalling on the Euston–Watford line is replaced by new equipment which is commissioned today. Seventy modern signals replace 100 of the old ones on this busy route.

12. PRESERVED. Stanier 2–6–4Ts exchange at Lakeside and Haverthwaite Railway.

16. SPRINTERS GROUNDED. The entire fleet of 42 Class 155 Sprinters are taken out of traffic because of door problems.

20. LONDON UNDERGROUND. The Minister of State for Transport announces an increase from 350 to 400 officers for the London Underground Division of the British Transport Police.

20. CATERING. Travellers Fare Ltd. is sold for £20.5 m to a management buy-out team following competive tendering. British Rail will receive rent for the use of the 270 catering units at over 140 stations.

21. SETTLE–CARLISLE LINE. The Joint County Councils submit 'Settle–Carlisle Railway: The Case for Retention' to Michael Portillo. The Councils claim that the government had compromised its position by announcing it was "minded" to consent to closure and directing BR to sell the line before deciding over the closure application.

31. CHANNEL TUNNEL. Seven km of tunnelling on English and French sides at year's end is achieved. During 1988, £551 m is the cost incurred (net of investment income).

31. ROAD CONGESTION. By year's end there are 23.3 m vehicles licensed in Britain, up 5% on 1987. Of these 18.9 m are private cars, and of these 2.45 m are company cars. For the first time since motorway-building began, no new extra miles of motorway were added to the network during the year.

31. GRAFFITI. This craze, imported from the United States, is estimated to have cost BR over £3 m during 1988.

▲With the start of the winter timetable on 3rd October, Bradford Forster Square was able to offer direct InterCity services to London King's Cross. The official reason for the switch from Bradford Interchange to Forster Square was to serve Shipley. The real reason was that when running with an electric loco at one end and an HST power car on the other, the single HST power car would be unable to get up the bank out of Bradford Interchange station. An unidentified Class 43 power car heads the Sundays only 12.42 Bradford Forster Square–London King's Cross on 20th November. *Les Nixon*

BR STOCK CHANGES 1988

LOCOMOTIVES

New Locomotives

March:

90005

April:

90001 90003 90007 91002
90002 90004 91001 91003

May:

89001 90008 91005

June:

91004 91006

July:

91007 91008

August:

91009

September:

90006 90009 90011 90010

October:

90014

November:

90012 90013 90015

December:

90016 90017 90018

Locomotives Reinstated

January:

33012

February:

33038

March:

31161 31323

May:

47104 83012

August:

03179 45106

November:

08309 33202 47145 47189
33025

Locomotives Withdrawn

January:

03066 08141 33034 47093
03078 08191 45124 47113
03094 33017

February:

08206 08779 33025 45150
08361 20002 33202 47106
08461 20161 45033 47140
08487 31195 45145 83015
08606 33018

March:

08102 31109 33049 81003
08168 31161 45140 81008
08331 31401 47130 81014
20180 33001

April:

08406 08626 31218 47104
08408 20001 33010 50013
08456 20152 40122 50047
08478 20174 45104

May:

08295 20077 47159 47192
08764 47145 47189 85029
20076

June:

08621 45052 45115 47104
45041

July:

08224 31183 45037 45110
08395 45007 45106 47713
08943 45012 45107

August:

08297 08852 45103 45128
08458 20022 45113 45141
08494 45046

September:

08210 08503 31121 50010
08285 08774 31167 50022
08367 20086 33038 50038
08385 20201 33059 81006
08420 20226

October:

08177 08439 08639 31222
08296 08459 08678 31280
08305 08502 26029 33028
08309 08504 31202

November:

08250 08579 08716 20209
08258 08608 20041 33112
08423 08640 20060 47235
08468 08671 20101 47342

December:

08898 20203 31227 47487
20146 31143 33209

Locos. Withdrawn from Departmental Service:

March:

ADB 968000

July:

97409 97411

August:

97410 97413
97412 ADB 968026

Undated:

ADB 968024

Locos. Renumbered

From	*To*	From	To
31161	31400	37193	37375
37008	37352	37199	37376
37014	37709	37200	37377
37021	37115	37204	37378
37024	37114	37226	37379
37032	37353	37257	37668
37043	37354	37259	37380
37044	37710	37284	37381
37045	37355	37314	37190
37052	37713	37322	37049
37068	37356	47497	47717
37079	37357	73102	73212
37085	37711	73113	73211
37089	37708	73116	73210
37091	37358	73120	73209
37102	37712	73121	73208
37117	37521	73122	73207
37118	37359	73123	73206
37119	37350	73124	73205
37127	37370	73125	73204
37147	37371	73127	73203
37151	37667	73137	73202
37159	37372	73142	73201
37160	37373	86205	86503
37165	37374	86217	86504
37176	37883	86222	86502
37177	37885	86239	86507
37180	37886	86246	86505
37183	37884	86258	86501

▼All class 45s were withdrawn by August 1988. Two of the last in service Nos. 45106 (later reinstated) and 45107 are seen at Derby on 25th May. *Graham Scott-Lowe*

Locomotives Transferred to Departmental Status and Renumbered

September:

From	*To*	From	To
47472	97472	47545	97545
47480	97480	47561	97561

COACHING STOCK

Coaches Withdrawn

January:

5223 13412

February:

1705 5117 13410 18713
1713 5305 13552 18842
1727 7220 18363 18932
3829 7632 18409 35060
3840 7996 18659 35130
5102

March:

1508 1881 5571 18895
1524 3021 5583 18929
1554 3051 6404 19533
1563 3055 6408 19535
1567 3063 6411 19538
1702 3075 6416 19541
1704 3093 7169 19544
1706 3824 7180 19546
1707 3833 7183 19547
1708 5079 9470 21238
1709 5082 13425 21243
1711 5083 13453 24835
1725 5115 13539 34533
1729 5126 13542 34557
1730 5129 17107 34638
1731 5130 18283 34641
1738 5504 18292 34642
1740 5514 18296 34671
1747 5535 18372 35045
1750 5543 18413 35073
1753 5545 18572 35119
1758 5555 18650 35286
1877 5559 18725

April:

5188

May:

5071 18928 34627 35042
5127 18961 34925 35044
7194 18964 34935 35063
13477 18969 34937 35192
13492 18971 34941 35193
13559 18995 34949 35196
18625 34556 34951 35200
18816 34624 34953 35318
18919 34625

June:

3953 18360 18740 35066
4808 18371 18882 35180
5095 18375 19001 35199
5238 18376 24585 35206
6505 18612 34547 35322
9415 18723 34623 35326
17087

July:

1513 | 18618 | 18782 | 18976
7207 | 18619 | 18786 | 19483
7225 | 18631 | 18812 | 19560
7234 | 18705 | 18827 | 34666
17018 | 18712 | 18861 | 35122
17019 | 18719 | 18923 | 35183
17033 | 18734 | 18949 | 35203
18250 | 18735 | 18963 | 35280
18599 | 18741 | 18966 | 35324
18609

August:

5098 | 5122 | 18330 | 18993
5101 | 13417 | 18613 | 35011
5119 | 13419 | 18773 | 35191
5121

September:

6412 | 18373 | 18982 | 35074
7208 | 18595 | 19021 | 35190
9007 | 18721 | 34529 | 35310
13468 | 18751 | 35064

Coaches Reinstated

July:

5309 | 5376 | 5378

August:

5389

September:

21238

November:

35456

Coaches Renumbered

From	*To*	From	To
3291	1203	6438	1205
3302	1216	6444	1217
3305	1211	6445	1201
3319	1206	6453	1212
3332	1218	6456	1202
3341	6704	6457	1209
3371	1221	6459	1200
3377	1215	6462	1210
3393	1208	21267	2834
3401	1204	21270	2833
3418	1219	35291	80224*
3419	1213	35295	80216*
3421	6702	35327	80225*
3605	3136	35328	80221*
3606	3606	35331	80223*
3608	3141	35501	17092
6422	1207	35502	17089
6432	1220	35503	17090
6433	1214		

* Converted to NPCCS.

DIESEL MULTIPLE UNITS

New DMUs

January:

155 310 | 155 313 | 156 402
155 311 | 155 314 | 156 403

February:

155 315 | 155 319 | 156 404
155 316 | 155 320 | 156 405
155 317 | 155 321 | 156 406
155 318

March:

155 322 | 155 323 | 155 324
155 325 | 156 411 | 55854
155 326 | 156 412 | 55855
156 407 | 55850 | 55856
156 408 | 55851 | 55857
156 409 | 55852 | 55858
156 410 | 55853 | 55859

April:

155 327 | 156 413 | 156 414
155 328

May:

155 329 | 155 334 | 156 418
155 330 | 156 415 | 156 420
155 331 | 156 416 | 156 421
155 332 | 156 417 | 156 422

June:

155 312 | 156 419 | 156 425
155 333 | 156 423 | 156 426
155 335 | 156 424 | 156 427

July:

155 341 | 156 429 | 156 432
156 428

August:

155 342 | 156 433 | 156 435
156 430 | 156 434 | 156 436
156 431

September:

155 343 | 156 437 | 156 440
155 344 | 156 438 | 156 441
155 345 | 156 439 | 156 442

October:

155 346 | 156 444 | 156 446
155 347 | 156 445 | 156 447
156 443

November:

156 448 | 156 452 | 156 456
156 449 | 156 453 | 156 457
156 450 | 156 454 | 156 458
156 451 | 156 455

December:

156 459 | 156 462 | 156 465
156 460 | 156 463 | 156 466
156 461 | 156 464

DMUs Reinstated

January:

51069 | 53078 | 53117 | 59037
51097 | 53109 | 59035 | 59041
53059

February:

59428

March:

59096 | 59116

June:

54026

July:

59097 | 59124 | 59532

November:

53746

DMUs Withdrawn

January:

51054 | 51313 | 53052 | 53108
51080 | 51328 | 53075 | 53206
53262 | 53896 | 59423 | 59568
53424 | 53905 | 59426 | 60103
53434 | 54005 | 59432 | 60121
53819 | 59329 | 59434 | 60807
53835 | 59345 | 59527 | 60121
53884 | 59374

February:

52073 | 53833 | 54250 | 59541
53003 | 54002 | 59119 | 59552
53023 | 54022 | 59415 | 59714
53100 | 54029

March:

51052 | 51323 | 53871 | 59096
51059 | 51324 | 53914 | 59120
51078 | 53063 | 54069 | 59364
51082 | 53065 | 54074 | 59560
51083 | 53070 | 54077 | 59563
51087 | 53077 | 54083 | 59626
51102 | 53095 | 54089 | 59636
51106 | 53119 | 54177 | 59638
51303 | 53120 | 54404 | 59642
51308 | 53121 | 54406 | 59650
51309 | 53205 | 59054 | 60044
51318 | 53227 | 59096

April:

51248 | 59048 | 59116 | 59262
53292 | 59060 | 59124 | 59524
59046 | 59097 | 59215 | 59532

May:

51587 | 53133 | 53913 | 59471
53041 | 53703 | 59035 | 59477
53051 | 53713 | 59037 | 59686
53072 | 53900 | 59041 | 59687
53123 | 53901 | 59372 | 59689

June:

53001 | 53033 | 53906 | 59112
53007 | 53042 | 53967 | 59375
53009 | 53043 | 54004 | 59649
53011 | 53045 | 54007 | 60018
53012 | 53047 | 54018 | 60019
53013 | 53129 | 54023 | 60527
53014 | 53654 | 54037 | 60528
53022 | 53825 | 54038 | 60529
53025 | 53869 | 54040 | 60709
53031 | 53872 | 54044

July:

51063 | 51322 | 51845 | 59078
51069 | 51457 | 53234 | 59122
51097 | 51802 | 53832 | 59428
51302 | 51818 | 53842 | 59528
51317

August:

51055 | 51056 | 51100

September:

51058 | 53610 | 54090 | 59344
51232 | 53746 | 54364 | 59418
51537 | 53746 | 59045 | 59555
53017 | 53839 | 59052 | 59556
53024 | 54014 | 59075 | 59564
53258 | 54033 | 59114 | 59692
53369 | 54078 | 59123

October:

51209 | 53166 | 53867 | 53920
51527 | 53217 | 53895 | 59230
51826 | 53856 | 53904 | 59433
52076 | 53862 | 53909 | 59554
53081

November:

51091 | 53078 | 53220 | 54122
51214 | 53109 | 53252 | 59039
51250 | 53117 | 53261 | 59414
51464 | 53161 | 53359 | 59422
51525 | 53178 | 53870 | 59469
51526 | 53191 | 53923 | 59479
53059

December:

51204 | 53091 | 53847 | 59282
51229 | 53747 | 53910 | 59475
51824 | 53749 | 54281 | 60521
51838 | 53750 | 59069 | 60707
53087

DMUs Renumbered

From	*To*
51464	TDB 977607†
51525	TDB 977608†
51824	TDB 977611†
51826	TDB 977613†
51838	TDB 977612†
52076	TDB 977614†
54281	TDB 977615†
54367	6301*
60300	67300§
60301	67301§
60400	67400§
60401	67401§

† To departmental stock.
* To hauled stock.
§ To EMU.

Departmental DMU Vehicles Withdrawn

Undated:

TDB 975537 | TDB 977223
TDB 975538 | TDB 977453
TDB 975964 | TDB 977454
TDB 975994 | TDB 977539
TDB 977049 | TDB 977540

ELECTRIC MULTIPLE UNITS

New EMUs

January:

319 011 | 319 013 | 319 016
319 012 | 319 014

February:

2402 | 319 019 | 319 023
319 015 | 319 020 | 319 024
319 017 | 319 021 | 319 025
319 018 | 319 022

March:

2403 | 319 028 | 319 031
319 026 | 319 029 | 319 032
319 027 | 319 030 | 319 033

April:

2404 | 319 034 | 319 036
2405 | 319 035 | 319 037

May:

2406 | 319 038 | 319 043
2407 | 319 039 | 319 045
2408 | 319 040 | 319 046
2409 | 319 041 | 319 047
2410 | 319 042

June:

319 044 | 319 048

July:

2411 | 2414 | 319 051
2412 | 319 049 | 319 052
2413 | 319 050 | 319 053

August:

2415 | 319 054 | 319 057
2416 | 319 055 | 319 058
2417 | 319 056

September:

2418 | 2419

October:

2420 | 319 059

November:

2401 | 321 303 | 321 305
2421 | 321 304 | 321 307
319 060

Vehicles Withdrawn

January:

61511 | 75239 | 75633 | 76412
62167 | 75314 | 75761 | 76424
62172 | 75598 | 76407

March:

14280 | 15365

April:

15 | 61495 | 75098 | 75421
20 | 61498 | 75206 | 75580
61073 | 65403 | 75212 | 75583
61092 | 70073 | 75336 | 75618
61221 | 75061 | 75353 | 75810
61285 | 75074 | 75405 | 77125
61301 | 75080

May:

62167 | 76407 | 76426

June:

61506 | 62156 | 62479 | 70804
61857 | 62157 | 62480 | 70805
62143 | 62158 | 62481 | 70809
62144 | 62159 | 69320 | 70811
62147 | 62160 | 69322 | 71159
62148 | 62161 | 69323 | 75591
62150 | 62162 | 69324 | 75615
62151 | 62476 | 69328 | 75791
62152 | 62477 | 69329 | 75847
62155 | 62478 | 70802

July:

76429

September:

61062 | 61228 | 72601 | 75213
61086 | 61510 | 72700 | 75215
61089 | 61827 | 75035 | 75282
61099 | 70089 | 75070 | 75317
61125 | 70097 | 75077 | 75319
61195 | 70101 | 75203 | 75335
61210 | 70199 | 75211 | 75630

October:

43 | 70813 | 70843 | 71158
92 | 70814 | 70845 | 71161
93 | 70819 | 70851 | 71162
94 | 70822 | 70852 | 71165
95 | 70824 | 70856 | 71166
61820 | 70827 | 70859 | 71167
69319 | 70833 | 70862 | 75754
69326 | 70835 | 70865 | 75778
70801 | 70836 | 70867 | 76271
70808 | 70840 | 70868 | 76272
70810 | 70841 | 71157 | 76273
76274 | 76298 | 76315 | 76327
76283 | 76299 | 76316 | 76328
76289 | 76305 | 76317 | 76943
76290 | 76306 | 76318 | 76944
76293 | 76311 | 76325 | 76947
76294 | 76312 | 76326 | 76948

November:

61101 | 70215 | 75196 | 75286
70062 | 75087 | 75244 | 75287
70082 | 75098 | 75267 | 75288
70121

December:

75928

Vehicles Reinstated

September:

76429

EMUs Renumbered to Departmental Stock

From	*To*
61052	ADB 977605
61073	ADB 977599
61228	ADB 977602
65414	ADB 977609
75035	ADB 977603
75070	ADB 977606
75077	ADB 977604
75080	ADB 977598
75211	ADB 977601
76061	ADB 977600
77101	ADB 977578
77109	ADB 977579
77136	ADB 977610

Departmental EMU Vehicles Withdrawn

Undated:

ADB 977207 | ADB 977212
ADB 977208 | ADB 977307
ADB 977209 | ADB 977308
ADB 977210 | ADB 977309
ADB 977211

NON-PASSENGER-CARRYING COACHING STOCK

NPCCS Withdrawn

January:

80503 | 84014 | 84625 | 93574
80525 | 84603 | 93159 | 93665

February:

80727 | 93337 | 93736 | 93949
93168

March:

80651 | 84586 | 93094 | 93975
80813 | 84587 | 93580 | 94698
84196 | 84594 | 93599 | 96294
84573 | 84605 | 93626 | 96299
84575 | 84612 | 93928 | 99652
84578 | 84616 | 93945 | 99653
84579 | 84628

April:

80515 | 84341 | 93286 | 93734

May:

80849

June:

80526 | 80553 | 80556 | 80559
80579 | 80814 | 84125 | 93320
80602 | 80828 | 84168 | 93351
80638 | 80862 | 84199 | 93592
80648 | 80896 | 84333 | 93707
80655 | 80905 | 84358 | 93786
80665 | 84028 | 84368 | 93968
80678 | 84056 | 84545 | 94067
80705 | 84067 | 93208 | 94899
80758 | 84097

July:

80507 | 93157 | 93492 | 93850
80529 | 93169 | 93497 | 93866
80547 | 93181 | 93509 | 93870
80594 | 93213 | 93526 | 93900
80597 | 93218 | 93527 | 93903
80611 | 93222 | 93531 | 93912
80619 | 93226 | 93545 | 93916
80632 | 93227 | 93553 | 93924
80706 | 93229 | 93555 | 93954
80708 | 93231 | 93559 | 93963
80712 | 93233 | 93564 | 93965
80726 | 93237 | 93565 | 93972
80823 | 93238 | 93566 | 93984
80840 | 93240 | 93575 | 94054
80844 | 93245 | 93584 | 94055
80986 | 93248 | 93586 | 94059
84003 | 93256 | 93587 | 94060
84017 | 93259 | 93588 | 94063
84039 | 93260 | 93593 | 94064
84040 | 93279 | 93598 | 94065
84050 | 93296 | 93612 | 94066
84072 | 93302 | 93615 | 94069
84096 | 93309 | 93619 | 94070
84127 | 93312 | 93625 | 94072
84130 | 93316 | 93642 | 94073
84141 | 93332 | 93670 | 94074
84144 | 93341 | 93678 | 94112
84278 | 93346 | 93693 | 94173
84288 | 93352 | 93699 | 94176
84291 | 93364 | 93737 | 94219
84338 | 93384 | 93754 | 94239
84369 | 93387 | 93761 | 94298
84417 | 93397 | 93766 | 94303
84468 | 93436 | 93772 | 94307
84564 | 93439 | 93776 | 94314
84571 | 93441 | 93787 | 94335
93102 | 93445 | 93789 | 94458
93111 | 93449 | 93797 | 94520
93125 | 93451 | 93799 | 94590
93129 | 93470 | 93805 | 94792
93132 | 93473 | 93808 | 94817
93147 | 93481 | 93817 | 94892
93152 | 93487 | 93819 | 94919

August:

80520 | 84180 | 93315 | 93645
80543 | 84359 | 93322 | 93662
80584 | 84384 | 93383 | 93688
80586 | 84437 | 93423 | 93702
80640 | 93096 | 93428 | 93813
80711 | 93113 | 93433 | 93825
80724 | 93128 | 93435 | 93827
80793 | 93149 | 93469 | 93878
84032 | 93158 | 93483 | 93885
84079 | 93161 | 93491 | 93938
84092 | 93219 | 93513 | 93953
84094 | 93246 | 93632 | 93960
84126 | 93264

September:

84379 | 93420 | 93639 | 94783
93230

October:

80757 | 93197 | 93899 | 99654
84095 | 93654 | 99609 | 99655
84269 | 93697 | 99610 | 99656
84441 | 93698 | 99638 | 99660
84544 | 93773

November:

80656 | 80735

NPCCS Reinstated

August:

84141 | 93776

December:

80651

NPCCS Renumbered

From	*To*	From	To
80503	95312	93337	96156
80525	95321	93351	96158
84014	95332	93665	96191
84341	95329	93734	96100
93159	96170	93736	96130
93168	96187	93737	96131
93286	96151	93754	96132
93320	96188	93949	96194

▼Previously-named Class 50 No. 50149 *Defiance*, was twinned with the naval establishment of the same name on 17th July at Laira – the occasion of the depot's open day. The new embellishment and nameplate are seen with curtains drawn back, following the unveiling.
Colin J Marsden

BR NAMINGS & DENAMINGS

LOCOMOTIVES NAMED DURING 1988

JANUARY

16	47231	The Silcock Express	Liverpool Lime St

FEBRUARY

23	43093	York Festival '88	York
24	37511	Stockton Haulage	Stockton

MARCH

03	47319	Norsk Hydro	Immingham Terminal
04	73131	County Of Surrey	Haslemere
17	58002	Daw Mill Colliery	Daw Mill Colliery
30	90005	Financial Times	London Euston

APRIL

10	09012	Dick Hardy	Stewarts Lane TMD
13	37358	P & O Containers	Southampton
14	56122	Wilton – Coalpower	Middlesbrough
22	31413	Severn Valley Railway	Kidderminster
23	31428	North Yorkshire Moors Railway	Grosmont 30
	33114	Sultan	Eastleigh Depot

MAY

02	08631	Eagle	Cambridge
02	08772	CAMULODUNUM	Colchester Depot
03	43147	Red Cross	London Paddington
11	73138	Post Haste 150 YEARS OF TRAVELLING POST OFFICES	Tonbridge
16	33050	Isle of Grain	Isle of Grain
16	33051	Shakespeare Cliff	Isle of Grain
18	37423	Sir Murray Morrison 1874–1948 Pioneer Of British Aluminium Industry	British Alcan, Fort William
21	43103	John Wesley	London St. Pancras
21	43118	Charles Wesley	London St. Pancras
21	58018	High Marnham Power Station	High Marnham
27	37888	Perolea	Stratford TMD

JUNE

11	56123	Drax Power Station	Drax
11	58014	Didcot Power Station	Didcot
16	47434	Pride In Huddersfield	Huddersfield
23	37688	Great Rocks	ICI Hindlow
30	47311	Warrington Yard	Warrington
	37320	Shap Fell	Motherwell
	73130	City of Portsmouth	Portsmouth

JULY

12	43186	Sir Francis Drake	Plymouth
14	47588	Carlisle Currock	Carlisle
	47317	Willesden Yard	Willesden
	47452	Aycliffe	Crewe Diesel Depot

AUGUST

03	47604	Womens' Royal Voluntary Service	Glasgow Central
09	47488	Rail Riders	Crewe Diesel Depot
15	47119	Arcidae	Crewe Diesel Depot
17	31444	Keighley & Worth Valley Railway	Keighley
	47085	Conidae	Crewe Diesel Depot
	47125	Tonnidae	Crewe Diesel Depot
	47190	Pectinidae	Crewe Diesel Depot
	47193	Lucinidae	Crewe Diesel Depot
	47194	Bullidae	Crewe Diesel Depot
	47195	Muricidae	Crewe Diesel Depot
	47324	Glossidae	Crewe Diesel Depot
	47368	Neritidae	Crewe Diesel depot
	47503	The Geordie	Crewe Diesel Depot

SEPTEMBER

10	56028	West Burton Power Station	West Burton PS
10	73005	Mid hants Watercress Line	
11	47283	Johnnie Walker	Kilmarnock
21	37698	Coedbach	Coed Bach Washery
22	47490	Bristol Bath Road	Bristol Bath Road TMD
26	37059	Port of Tilbury	Tilbury Riverside
27	43149	BBC Wales Today	Cardiff Central
	37667	Wensleydale	Thornaby TMD
	37668	Leyburn	Thornaby TMD
	47717	Tayside Region	Doncaster Major Depot

OCTOBER

04	43150	Bristol Evening Post	Bristol Temple Meads
07	47060	Halewood Silver Jubilee 1988	Liverpool Lime Street
09	31430	Sister Dora	Bescot TMD
09	47238	Bescot Yard	Bescot
10	90011	The Chartered Institute of Transport	London Euston
12	43191	Seahawk	Plymouth
12	43192	City of Truro	
	47198	Haliotidae	Crewe Diesel Depot
	47233	Strombidae	Crewe Diesel Depot
	47278	Vasidae	Crewe Diesel Depot
	47424	The Brontës of Haworth	Crewe Diesel Depot

NOVEMBER

09	37711	Tremorfa Steel Works	Cardiff Tidal Sidings
09	37712	The Cardiff Rod Mill	Cardiff Tidal Sidings
10	87012	The Royal Bank of Scotland	London Euston
	37403	Glendarroch	Eastfield TMD
	47010	Xancidae	Crewe Diesel TMD
	58003	Markham Colliery	Markham Colliery

DECEMBER

01	31276	Calder Hall Power Station	Sellafield
16	37275	Stainless Pioneer	Tinsley Yard
	87006	City of Glasgow	Willesden TMD

LOCOMOTIVE NAMES REMOVED DURING 1988

FEBRUARY

43092	Highland Chieftain

MARCH

43105	Hartlepool
43194	Royal Signals

MAY

43061	City of Lincoln
47401	North Eastern
47406	Rail Riders
47407	Aycliffe
47411	The Geordie

SEPTEMBER

43121	West Yorkshire Metropolitan County
47639	Industry Year 1986

OCTOBER

37229	The Cardiff Rod Mill

NOVEMBER

37403	Isle of Mull

DECEMBER

43091	Edinburgh Military Tattoo
43107	City of Derby
43110	Darlington
87006	Glasgow Garden Festival

UNDATED

37320	Shap Fell
37409	Loch Awe
37424	Glendarroch
43002	Top of the Pops
43013	University of Bristol
43131	Sir Felix Pole
43142	St. Mary's Hospital, Paddington
43186	City of Plymouth
47374	Petrolea
47402	Gateshead
47421	The Brontës of Haworth
47526	Northumbria
47625	CITY OF TRURO
87016	Sir Francis Drake